FORWARD

The First American

Unsupported Expedition

to the North Pole

FORWARD

George —
To the expedition life!
All the best

John Huston and
Tyler Fish

John M. Huston

OCTANE
PRESS

Boulder, Co — June 25, 2020

Octane Press, First Edition, December 2011
Second Printing, June 2013
Copyright © by John Huston and Tyler Fish

ISBN 978-1-937747-90-9

Book design by Diana Boger
Content edit by Randal Hendee
Expedition map data by Tim Harincar
Map design by Kirk Lyttle
Proof by Charles Everitt and Zac Thompson

Opposite title page: Crumple zone. Sunset, Day 18.

northpole09.com
John Huston: john@forwardendeavors.com
Tyler Fish: tyler@forwardexpeditions.com

Library of Congress Cataloging-in-Publication Data

Huston, John, 1976– and Fish, Tyler, 1973–

Forward: The First American Unsupported Expedition to the North Pole /
    John Huston and Tyler Fish.

1. North Pole—Exploration and expeditions.
2. Arctic Ocean—Travel and exploration.
3. Polar exploration—North Pole and unsupported expeditions.
    Canadian Arctic—Travel and description.
4. Huston, John, 1976– —Polar exploration—North Pole.
5. Fish, Tyler, 1973– —Polar exploration—North Pole.

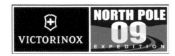

Printed in China by Nordica.

This book is dedicated to our families,
our expedition teammates for life.

Contents

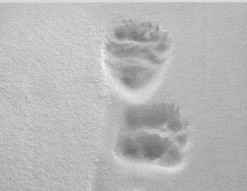

EXPEDITION INSIGHTS

1 ICY PANTS

By John Huston with Chris Niskanen

The view south, Day 47, 9:00 a.m. Tyler follows John's tracks with the morning sun behind him.

"Anyone who has never made a mistake has never tried anything new." —Albert Einstein

We stand atop a frozen sea that stretches out before us. For these past forty-seven days it has been our constant companion and our home. We have skied, snowshoed, and sometimes even swum toward the North Pole, climbing over ridges and threading our way among ice boulders large and small. In our backpacks and in Kevlar sleds called pulks, we carry or haul everything we need to sustain us on our journey: food, clothes, tents, navigation gear, and satellite phones. No Americans have ever traveled under their own power to the North Pole without resupply. We hope to be the first.

In the next few days we expect to begin an all-out race to the Pole. We have 103 nautical miles (nm)* left to go. A Russian helicopter is scheduled to pick us up in eight days. If we don't meet this deadline, we fail.

It is April 17, the spring season on the Arctic Ocean. This morning at 5:00, like every other morning of our trip, we rose from our down-insulated sleeping bags

---

*1 nautical mile = 1.15 statute miles (street miles). In this text nautical mile is abbreviated "nm." The distance from the northernmost point of Canada to the North Pole is 416 nm or about 479 statute miles. Due to our meandering route and the southward drift of sea ice, we actually need to cover more than 445 nm or more than 512 statute miles.

The view north, Day 47, 9:00 a.m. Excellent skiing conditions. John picks out a landmark.

John Huston, age 32.

Tyler Fish, age 35.

and quietly prepared for another day on the ice. With daylight lasting twenty-four hours, the tent was bathed in sunlight as we fixed our breakfast by thawing out a block of pemmican—a mixture of meat, fat, vegetables, and spices. A half-stick of butter topped off our fatty stew. We have come to love eating chunks of butter and deep-fried bacon, two staples of the super diet that keeps us alive. Hauling our heavy loads in this brutal cold means we need to consume calories at the phenomenal rate of at least seven hundred per hour, almost four times the norm for a person walking, say, along Lake Michigan on a November morning.

Our thermometer this morning read -34° Fahrenheit. Now, four hours later, the temperature has risen to a balmy -10° F.

We eat, sleep, and ski. Sometimes we climb over chunks of ice the size of Volkswagens. To cross short stretches of open water we put on waterproof suits called drysuits and swim through slushy seawater, towing our floatable pulks behind us.

At this moment my blood is warm and my mind awash with problems, some technical and some personal. We halt at the edge of a lead—a gap in the sea ice— which froze over maybe a day or two before.

Floating on the Arctic Ocean are giant plates of ice that constantly move and grind against one another. Stretches of water called "open leads" are formed when these plates pull apart. Open leads sometimes look like small rivers or creeks with no current. Eventually, these leads will refreeze, but with a thinner layer of ice.

I am staring at the ice in this lead, wondering if it will support my weight and the one hundred pounds of gear in my pulk. The lead is dark and speckled with frost flowers an inch high. Dark ice is new ice. I hope it will hold us. The ocean below is two and a half miles deep.

I punch the ice with the tip of my ski pole. It doesn't poke through. The rule of thumb: If the ice doesn't give after three good jabs, it's usually solid enough to ski across.

"It looks like the same ice we skied over yesterday," Tyler calls out over the wind. "It looks good."

Tyler Fish is thirty-five years old, a powerful and skilled cross-country skier, and my partner on this 416-nm journey to the Pole. A ruff of wolverine fur, heavily encrusted with frost, frames his bearded, weather-roughened face. His wife Sarah and infant son Ethan are waiting for him back home in Ely, Minnesota.

Tyler, afternoon of Day 46.

Tyler and I trust each other implicitly, but lately our relationship has had its tensions. We've known each other for nine years, since our days working together at Outward Bound, the famous outdoor leadership school. Now, we are like soldiers marching through a moonscape of ice, dependent on each other for survival. Our ability to excel as a team, assessing our progress and mulling over each predicament we face, will determine the success of our mission.

This morning, after months of simmering and silent complaints, Tyler released his pent-up frustrations in a reflective rant that lasted close to thirty minutes. I listened to him as a friend who knows he should just listen. He is a good man, the clear-headed sort you want in a tight spot in the Arctic. I trust him with my life, and I know that his venting will clear the air and make us stronger. Still, I feel blindsided and a bit distracted. I wish I could just call up my girlfriend Jennifer and talk it through with her.

Newly frozen leads are exciting but treacherous. When we ski up to a lead, it

The lead.

always makes us slow down and think. If the crossing goes smoothly, we're on our way. If we screw up, we're in the ocean, in a race for survival.

After a few more jabs at the ice with my pole, I agree with Tyler. "Yeah. Yesterday we walked over ice like this."

I'm standing on the apron of the newly frozen lead. The ice here is white and solid. I shove off and begin to slide toward the dark ice. We always move fast across a lead, so I put some muscle into my stride. Right away I sense that something is horribly wrong.

Puddles appear on the ice. I feel myself skiing downward as the ice beneath my skis begins to sink.

It's as if I'm on an escalator, slowly descending into the abyss. There is no turning back as water begins to swallow me.

"John, you're going in! Ski faster!"

I'm about thirty feet in front of Tyler. I try to ski faster, but I keep sinking. My brain grasps the inevitable: I'm going to have to swim.

"I'm okay. I'm okay," I yell back to Tyler. Now I'm in up to my neck in the ocean, awkwardly treading water while still gripping my ski poles.

I can't lose my skis! If my skis fall off, the expedition is doomed. The ocean water begins seeping through my clothes. At first it feels strangely warm, but after twenty seconds the piercing cold invades my hands, feet, and crotch.

My mind scrolls through the items I'm carrying. My camera is in one pocket, my compass and GPS in another. I'm wearing a backpack that contains our tent and a five-pound package of freeze-dried cheese. The backpack is tethered to my pulk, which now floats behind me.

Somehow the skis stay attached to my boots. I turn around and begin to struggle toward the apron of ice where Tyler is crouching.

Tyler pulls out our emergency throw bag, like the kind used in river rescues. He throws the bag but it falls well short. Now he is on his hands and knees, reaching to me with a ski pole.

"Grab on!" he yells. I just keep swimming.

The sound of his voice, the splashing water, the gusting wind—everything around me thunders in my ears. I can taste seawater.

Closer now, Tyler extends his hand.

"No," I say, fearing that if I grab it, I'll pull him in. Already there is water around his knees, as the apron threatens to give way. If we're both in the water, there will be no one to rescue either of us.

My body is already shunting blood toward my internal organs, the automatic reaction to impending hypothermia. I'm starting to panic, not from the fear of dying, but from the fear of frostbite.

Instead of grabbing his outstretched hand, I toss my poles toward him. I try pushing down on the edge of the apron, but chunks of it break away. After several more attempts, the ice finally holds. Like a swimmer at the edge of a pool, I haul my body up onto the frozen surface and awkwardly roll out of the water with my skis still attached.

My clothes hang in heavy, sopping folds as I stand up on my skis.

"Pole!"

Tyler hands me a ski pole so I can step away from the water and yank my sled onto the ice. We scramble away from the apron to where the ice is thicker.

"Dry clothes!" Sounds roar in my head.

Tyler is one step ahead of me. He is already into our sleds, digging out dry clothes. I shout out the names of articles I need as I peel them off. My mittens come off, then my outer layers. Tyler grabs a sleeping pad for me to stand on as he helps me pull off my boots.

I'm pulling my sopping wool underwear top over my head when it becomes stuck. I wrestle with it like a drunken man as the wind blasts my bare torso like a subzero blowtorch. Then I realize my watch is strapped to the outside of my sleeve, pinning the shirt to my wrist. It's all I can do to pull the rapidly stiffening shirt back on. I try to undo the clasp, but my fingers don't work.

"Watch!"

I'm down to one-word sentences. My hands and feet feel like daggers are pressing through them. I know frostbite is near.

Tyler fumbles to remove the watch. Finally, he takes off his liner mittens to undo the clasp. The cold metal against his thumb sears the skin. Once the watch is off and my final layer of wet clothes is on the ice, I begin putting on dry layers. Tyler lays down another pad for extra insulation and pulls out a sleeping bag. I slide into it and sit there with my knees drawn up to my chest. He wraps another sleeping bag around me. Then he hands me chocolate truffles, our instant energy source. I stuff them into my mouth.

Thirty minutes after John went through. Our throw bag lies on the apron of the newly frozen lead.

Frozen chaos. John's boots, long underwear, and pants—all frozen.

Mentally, I'm shutting down. I'm no longer thinking about Tyler's rant or the race to the Pole. I have to get warm and fuel my body. Even after wolfing down the truffles, I feel like I could eat every last crumb of pemmican left in our pulks.

For the first time, I feel completely helpless and unable to contribute. My only job now is to stave off hypothermia and frostbite. Tucked into my armpits, my hands come back pretty quickly. But I'm worried about my feet, which burn with cold. I take off my socks and insulated booties and hold my toes in my hands, trying to conduct heat into them. The wind continues to howl, buffeting my little cocoon of pads and sleeping bags.

Tyler has found a good place to set up the tent about forty yards away. When he returns fifteen minutes later, I jump out of the bag and sprint in my booties toward the tent with Tyler jogging after me carrying the sleeping bag and pads. I slide through the round tent door, relieved to be out of the wind. Tyler reaches in and passes me a few more truffles, which barely ease my raging hunger. I crawl into the sleeping bag while Tyler leaves to take pictures of our near catastrophe.

I savor the shelter of the tent until he returns to light our two stoves. We hang

Ice watch. John's Victorinox Swiss Army Night Vision II encased in frozen seawater after the swim.

my boot liners and mittens up to dry, but the inside of the tent is an icy mess. It's as if someone has dumped a gigantic Slurpee on the floor. Since we're on a tight ration of fuel, we're worried about dipping too deep into our reserves.

We nibble on nuts, truffles, and pieces of deep-fried bacon, quietly contemplating our next move. It's obvious we can't run the stoves long enough to dry everything without risking a fuel shortage. Nor do we have any time to spare.

"What do you think we should do?" I say, already knowing the answer.

"We need to keep going," Tyler says. "Today."

"I agree."

We know this is our only option. Tyler and I expected that one of us would go nineteen, my entire camping experience was limited to a few car trips with my parents and my Cub Scout troop.

My fondest winter memories of my early years are of my brother, sister, and I sledding down the big hill at the high school across the street from our house. Our father made it a point to teach us how to downhill ski. By age ten I was bombing down the modest slopes of Wisconsin and Michigan in a hell-bent tuck, not even thinking about turning. It was all or nothing. This mentality must have come from my father, a rugby player and entrepreneur who never did anything halfway. He has always been my biggest role model.

As an undergrad at Northwestern University, I tried to follow in Indy's footsteps. I studied archaeology, history, and geography. I got to be a team member on archaeological digs in New Mexico and northern Denmark and loved working outside in small teams. But in the end, I couldn't stomach the thought of a life of lab work and paper-writing.

As a freshman, I had joined the trial run of a backpacking and teambuilding program that took students hiking for a week before they arrived on campus in the fall. The program was based loosely on Outward Bound. Before the week was out, I was hooked. The next year I co-directed the program. Three years later I found myself standing on the back of a dogsled at -20° F on a frozen lake in the Boundary Waters of northern Minnesota, surrounded by pine trees. I was starting my career as an Outward Bound instructor in Ely, feeling like the luckiest man alive.

Simply put, I fell in love with winter and the North. From 2000 to 2005, I worked for Outward Bound year-round, sleeping outside more than two hundred nights a year. When I first met Tyler he came off as serious and nerdy in an endearing kind of way. He was a rock-solid instructor and paddler who spent almost all his time off with his girlfriend Sarah, who also worked at Outward Bound. I respected the way he carried himself, and I appreciated his compassion. He always thought deliberately about the way he impacted the people around him. Tyler was my supervisor for several of the courses I taught. Over the years we took occasional staff trips together where we shared in some unforgettable practical jokes.

In 2004, I skied the American Birkebeiner for the first time. The "Birkie" is the largest ski race in North America. Tyler came in 227th out of about six thousand that year, while I was happy just to finish the fifty-one-kilometer race. With guidance from Tyler, I soon integrated a few hours of training into my daily schedule. A

couple of years later I actually finished 227th as well, but I never caught up to him.

During the long winter nights in Ely, I spent my evenings sitting by the woodstove in my cabin on the lakeshore, devouring the literature of polar exploration. I was inspired by the optimism and determination of Ernest Shackleton. In 1914 he wrecked his ship in Antarctica but led his crew to safety, largely through the force of his positive personality. I was most drawn, however, to the non-harrowing polar adventures of lesser-known explorers such as Norwegians Fridtjof Nansen, Otto Sverdrup, and Roald Amundsen, the visionary who in 1911 led the first successful expedition to the South Pole. These men are less famous mainly because their expeditions were successful, well-planned affairs lacking the tragedy and high drama celebrated by the press and rehashed in history books. Plus, the Norwegian tendency toward understatement kept their feats relatively unknown outside their home country.

Amundsen's leadership genius became a beacon for me. I was drawn to his exhaustive approach to planning and his humble, self-critical passion for innovation and learning. I incorporated lessons from his legendary expeditions through the Northwest Passage and to the South Pole into my Outward Bound courses. I even named a sled-dog puppy after Lindstrom, Amundsen's comedic polar cook.

Roald Amundsen, polar genius.
Led the first expedition to the South Pole and the first expedition through the Northwest Passage. Known for his detailed and innovative planning, not for smiling in photographs.

Not many people get to walk in their heroes' shoes. But in the spring of 2005, a lightning bolt of fate enabled me to do just that. A British film company decided to replicate the 1911 race for the South Pole between the Norwegian Amundsen and the Englishman Robert F. Scott, with the resulting documentary to air on the BBC and The History Channel.

The producers planned to outfit two teams, one British and one Norwegian, in exactly the same manner as the historic expeditions. They chose Greenland as a venue because dogs and other non-

First to the South Pole. Roald Amundsen (far left) and his team at the South Pole, December 14, 1911.

indigenous animals are no longer permitted in Antarctica. A call was sent out for one American to join the Norwegians on the modern-day Amundsen team to facilitate a more fluid English conversation for the cameras. I cranked out the application in one cathartic night and left the next morning to lead a weeklong Outward Bound course. Two anxious weeks later I was chosen to serve as one of the two dog mushers on the team.

Rune Gjeldnes, one of the most accomplished polar explorers in the world, was our leader. Now a close friend and mentor, Rune holds the world records for the longest unsupported ski expeditions on the Arctic Ocean, Greenland, and Antarctica. Much like his predecessors, he is celebrated in Norway but little-known elsewhere.

Rune's optimism is a force of nature. He believes that a positive team vibe is absolutely essential for success. On the Greenland trip he outlawed complaining, and we joked and laughed all expedition long despite having to eat rotting pemmican

sprinkled with reindeer hair. Rune looks at an expedition as an inherently mental challenge, a test in which success is determined by the ability to control one's mental perspective. At this he is the master.

Over Amundsen-designed dinners of pemmican, seal meat, and seal blubber, Rune and I often talked about his epic 109-day expedition from Russia to the North Pole to Canada. The seal meat tasted like a blend of beefsteak and fish. We enjoyed that, but we struggled to choke down the disgusting pemmican.

During one of those dinners, about twenty days into the trip, Rune said, "You know, John, no American has ever skied to the North Pole unsupported. I think there is an opportunity for you there." I wasn't sure what to say. For the rest of that expedition and over the following year, I batted the idea around in my head. I was attracted to the challenge and the paths that it might open up in my life. At the same time, the thought of such a trip scared me.

Most of all, I was afraid of failing. I'd never traveled on the Arctic Ocean before, and I feared its reputation for dashing dreams and sometimes taking lives. The success rate for unsupported North Pole attempts was less than thirty-three

Rune Gjeldnes, polar superman.

percent. Added to the built-in hardships of living at -40° F, the thought of launching the project without a penny of seed money was truly frightening.

On the strength of Amundsen's methods and Rune's leadership, the modern Amundsen team crushed the modern Scott team. We won the race by more than six weeks and six hundred miles. I left Greenland ready to eat some normal food, thirsty for more polar expeditions, and once again feeling like the luckiest guy in the world.

In February 2007, I ran logistics for Global Warming 101, an educational expedition to

The Amundsen train. Four mushers, one skier, and forty-eight dogs head north on the Greenland ice cap, May 2005.

Brothers from another mother. (From left) John, Harald Kippenes, and Rune (our knuckles stained by seal blubber). The red tent gives the photo its tint.

Ninety-four years later, the modern Amundsen team. John is on the far left.

Baffin beauties. An Inuit sled dog team trots across a frozen lake on Baffin Island during the 2007 Global Warming 101 expedition.

Arctic Ocean the ski surface is stable. I'd be skiing on land covered by an ice cap that resembles an endless desert of snow. There would be a few crevasses to navigate around, but I wouldn't have to worry about the ice rubble, open leads, and sea-ice drift that come with a trip on the Arctic Ocean.

In late November 2007, my clients and I skied away from Hercules Inlet on the land edge of Antarctica. On Day 11, a massive cloud system shut out the sun.

When this happens on an ice cap, there is no horizon line. This is called whiteout, and it makes navigation exhausting. With nothing to focus on, skiing in straight lines is nearly impossible. It's like walking forward with your eyes closed, but instead of black you see white.

We caught glimpses of the sun on just four of the next sixteen days, and saw no sun at all for seven days straight. During this stretch it snowed two feet, which made it feel like we were pulling our sleds through mashed potatoes. The brutal weather put us

South Pole success. John and his two clients, Cameron Hudson and Sumiyo Tsuzuki, weary but happy.

Baffin Island run by native Elyite Will Steger. I lived in several remote coastal Inuit villages along the expedition team's dogsled route. The Inuits' hardiness and outdoor expertise were both humbling and awe-inspiring. And their keen sense of humor cracked me up. Before heading to the South Pole in 1910, Amundsen led a small team through the Northwest Passage. During that trip, he went out of his way to learn from the local Inuit populations, whom he saw as the true polar experts.

On Baffin Island I finally met Matty McNair, with whom I'd corresponded for several years. She lives in Iqaluit, the capital of Nunavut, Canada's Inuit-governed territory. Matty is a veteran of several North and South Pole expeditions and owns Northwinds Adventures, a polar guiding company. That spring, she hired me to lead a full-length ski expedition to the South Pole. This opportunity was the perfect steppingstone to the North Pole. Upon returning to Ely from Baffin Island in May 2007, I got ready to go south.

Antarctica is like a bigger, colder, windier version of Greenland. Unlike the

Whiteout. On the way to the South Pole. Whiteout days are really tough.

so far behind schedule that we had to ration our food before the resupply. We arrived at our halfway point, three hundred nautical miles, in thirty-seven days.

For the next twenty days we altered our sleep schedule to take advantage of the round-the-clock sunlight by operating on a twenty-eight-hour day instead of the normal twenty-four. This adjustment allowed us to ski longer hours and sleep less. Despite the mental slowness of sleep deprivation, the weight loss, and the unforgiving pangs of hunger, we pulled it off. On Day 57 we arrived at the South Pole, thoroughly worn out and bone-weary, but successful.

THE TEAM: TYLER FISH

As a small child I loved dinosaurs. The only thing I wanted to be was a paleontologist. I imagined myself digging up a long-lost prehistoric creature trapped in some undiscovered place. But marveling at the skeletons in the Science Museum of Minnesota was about as far as I got with that dream.

My parents tell me that the first time I stood on skis was during a trip to Red Lodge, Montana, when I was two. While I barely remember that event, I do recall the first time I really enjoyed skiing. I grew up in Minnesota, but my family chose to ski at Trollhaugen, a north-facing slope across the river in Wisconsin. My mom and dad would encourage me to sidestep up the hill and ski down. At first, I was doing it for my parents, just following their instructions. At some point I sidestepped higher up the hill and pointed my skis down the slope. As soon as I reached the bottom, I wanted to do it again. I was now doing it for me, not them. My future as a skier was set.

Before long, I was a junior racer, learning slalom and giant slalom and picking up speed. Initially, racing meant tears and frustration. Later on, it led to ribbons and even one regional championship. I was finished with downhill racing by the age of fourteen, but a few things stuck with me: valuable lessons of success and failure and lifelong friendships. As for the cold, I never shrank from it. I skied even on the coldest winter days. I would take a run, go in to warm up, take two more runs, and so on. It was just part of growing up.

I've always been an explorer, or at least a wanderer. As a child my imagination would walk with me as I crossed the street to check out the woods on the other side. I'd wander in one direction, then another, through woods and cornfields, until I finally popped out on the road and found my way home again. My parents tell a story about following my tracks in the snow on the way home from the bus stop a quarter-mile from our house (although I swear it was farther). Evidently, my tracks zigged and zagged through yards, over fences, and down to the lake. I'm sure I never knew where I was headed, but taking the long way home just seemed natural.

Wandering. Tyler, age six, on his grandparents' farm with their dog, Chubber.

Boundary Waters boy. Tyler, age eight, on a trip with his father in northern Minnesota.

Going downhill. Tyler speeds past a slalom gate, age twelve.

Peaceful paradise. The Boundary Waters at sunset.

© David J. Owen

My mom grew up on a farm twenty minutes from our house and my grandparents still lived there when I was a kid. That was an environment for some real exploring. I'd arrive at the farm, and after checking in with Grandma and eating the requisite cookies, I was off. Sometimes I was alone, but other times I'd walk with their beagle, Chubber. Together, we roamed about the farm, always looking and always finding. I don't remember what it was that we found. What I do know is that I was content.

When I was eight, my dad decided that he and I should go on a canoe trip in the Boundary Waters wilderness of northern Minnesota. I was thrilled with the idea, but by then I'd nearly drowned a few times, so I was nervous. Before we set out, my father made me use one of the pit toilets by the portage trail. That took the edge off, and the rest of my nervousness was swept away by the river, so much smaller and tamer than I expected.

That trip was momentous for me. There was cold and

Courtesy of Kim McIntyre, Voyageur Outward Bound School

Tyler teaching. An Outward Bound rock-climbing site near the Boundary Waters.

rain, my first walleye, a bear in camp, and a moose sighting. We enjoyed our time together, father and son. I was so proud of how I paddled—on the way out at least. I'm sure he was unimpressed by how little I paddled on the way back a few days later.

We started taking family trips every summer. Those trips turned into expeditions with friends, which became hiking trips in college with people I didn't know at first, but then got to know well. Out there in the wilderness, I could satisfy my natural curiosity and love for exercise, and the company was almost always good.

After graduating from Bates College in 1996, I began working for Outward Bound and I haven't left since. A six-week summer internship began in a dusty, musty cabin and a new life emerged, not just in the Boundary Waters, but on the rivers of Manitoba, the deserts of the Big Bend region of Texas, and, not least, on the frozen lakes of Minnesota and Ontario.

Paddle partners. Tyler and Sarah in a river rapid.

At Outward Bound I found a way to follow my passions and fully dedicate myself to a cause. There were some unexpected benefits as well. The people were great, and as I moved up the ranks, I learned more and more about running expeditions and facilitating groups through compassionate guidance. Outward Bound has nurtured my development as a leader, mentor, naturalist, counselor, risk manager, and lifelong learner.

In the summer of 1999 I met Sarah and thought nothing of it. Then in the fall we both worked for Outward Bound in Texas. Standing in the mud on the border of Texas and Mexico we talked and laughed. I felt something like, "Wow, she's great. How can I get our paths to cross again?" A few months later we hopped into her 1981 Volkswagen Vanagon and took off on a spring ski tour of the West.

It was love.

In 2004 Sarah and three other women from Outward Bound completed a 1,200-mile, ninety-eight-day dogsled trip across Canada. Their number one goal was to remain friends no matter what. It wasn't easy, but they succeeded. I was jealous of the scale of their expedition and wanted something like that for my own.

In 2005 I started my current position as director of the school's program for at-risk youth. Six weekends each summer I run seminars that challenge teenagers and parents to improve their relationships and reconsider their lives.

I got to know John in 2000 when he started working in Outward Bound's winter program. At first I thought he was a bit immature. His sense of humor didn't quite sync with mine, but I respected his enthusiasm for outdoor education. As I got to know him, I admired his willingness to learn and go after his goals. Soon we were traveling to ski races together.

When I wasn't working at Outward Bound I dedicated most of my time to racing. I loved everything about it: the speed, the culture, the Scandinavian connection, the complexity of the equipment, the intensity of the competition and the training of body and mind.

Several years ago I was asked to help coach the Ely High School Nordic ski team. I jumped at it. Coaches have had a big impact on my life. This was the perfect opportunity to combine my athletic talents with my ability to work with people.

When John brought up the North Pole idea, I didn't flinch. It sounded exciting, adventurous, long, difficult, and worth it. Long expeditions didn't bother me—usually, the longer the trip, the more I got into it. The physical hardships of the trip didn't scare me, either. I knew I could acquire the skills I didn't already have. What I paused at was the scope of it. What would it take to make it all happen?

Tyler looking speedy. The 2006 American Birkebeiner.

In the spring of 2006, the timing seemed right. I didn't own a house, wasn't married yet, and had no children. My life was uncomplicated. But that October Sarah and I got married. We bought a house the next year, and in the fall of 2008, Ethan was born.

BY JOHN HUSTON

"Outward Bound," according to its website, "is a non-profit educational organization and expedition school that serves people of all ages and backgrounds through active learning expeditions that inspire character development, self-discovery and service both in and out of the classroom." There are forty-two branches in thirty-three countries.

From the outset we believed that our three-year North Pole project would require a sound philosophical and interpersonal approach. For that we owe a great deal to the founding principles of Outward Bound. Tyler and I had spent years leading teams of students on strenuous expeditions, teaching technical skills, group communication, and collaboration along the way. Without that foundation, it would've been hard to imagine us working so well together on the ice.

Outward Bound was started in Britain in an effort to reduce casualties on merchant marine vessels torpedoed during World War II. The idea was to put young sailors through the moral equivalent of war, so they would gain confidence and tenacity without the ugliness of battle.

Over the next fifty years the organization grew to become the standard bearer for safety and quality in outdoor education. Outward Bound instructors emphasize both wilderness and leadership skills. By the end of most expeditions, students are able to travel independently in the wild.

As Outward Bound instructors, we were "brought up" to appreciate the discipline of physical fitness, the rigor of self-reliance, the value of craftsmanship, and the strength of compassion.

The Minnesota Outward Bound base camp, fifteen miles south of the town of Ely, sits next to the Boundary Waters Canoe Area Wilderness. Ely is a classic small town of four thousand. It has one main street, thirteen bars, at least as many outfitters, hundreds of lakefront cabins, and wilderness as its backyard.

Each summer 250,000 people visit Ely to enjoy the pure waters, extraordinary fishing, and endless canoe routes—and the mosquito hordes and backbreaking portages that come with them.

Many businesses shut their doors for the winter, when the town recedes beneath blankets of snow and frigid temperatures well below 0° F. Minus 20° F is common and -30° F not uncommon. One day in 1996 the thermometer reportedly hit -72° F!

Ely, Minnesota.
The main drag, early morning.

Canoe camp.
The Boundary Waters in the summer.

Courtesy of Tyler Sassaman

© David J. Owen

Courtesy of Outward Bound

Winter portage. A team of Outward Bound sled dogs. John's favorite lead dog, Boss Hog, is up front on the left.

Ely is home to a thriving cross-country ski culture and what has been called the largest concentration of sled dogs in the United States outside of Alaska. During the winter, when it's visited by only a few thousand people, the Boundary Waters area truly becomes a wilderness.

Perhaps it is the eccentric "can-do" mindset of most northwoods cabin dwellers that explains why several Ely residents have dogsledded to the North Pole and completed other polar expeditions. In 1986, Will Steger and Paul Schurke, both Elyites, led the first confirmed unresupplied expedition to the North Pole. Steger has led dogsled expeditions the length of Greenland, across Antarctica, and across the Arctic Ocean. He continues to organize expeditions and educational programs today.

In Ely, conversations in the ski and dogsled communities often turn to expedition stories and Arctic dreams.

Courtesy of Joe Bianco

Next generation. On winter Sundays, Ely's cross-country ski area is always crowded with kids.

BY JOHN HUSTON

CaringBridge is a nonprofit organization providing free websites that connect people experiencing a significant health challenge to family and friends. The mission of CaringBridge is to amplify the love, hope, and compassion in the world, making each health journey easier.

From the beginning, Tyler and I wanted our expedition to benefit a charity. Given our values of optimism, humility, and responsibility, CaringBridge was the perfect fit. Whether supporting a loved one through a health crisis or skiing to the North Pole, to us it's all about the mental side of challenge.

Each day over a half-million people connect through CaringBridge. Since it was founded in 1997, its personal websites have been visited over 1.7 billion times. The CaringBridge community includes authors, visitors, and donors from all fifty states and more than 225 countries and territories around the world.

In our minds, the challenges we faced on the ice were small compared to the challenges people deal with in times of health crisis. While traversing a field of snow waves or repeatedly struggling to warm up our hands, Tyler and I would often think of people who were facing bigger challenges, and how lucky we were to be following our dreams. These thoughts quickly squelched any complaining or self-pity.

We include CaringBridge.org in all of our interviews, presentations, and outreach. So far we've raised more than $11,000 for CaringBridge.

Courtesy of CaringBridge.org

"Why did I want to go to the North Pole? Fair enough question." —Tyler Fish

We get it all the time. We hear, "Why did you do it?" Or, "Why the hell would you want to do that?" We really don't like this question, but everyone keeps asking it. Our answers:

We see winter sport and travel as the ultimate wilderness experience. And we really, really love to cross-country ski.

We love having a daily physical training routine with a big goal as the focus. When we're on expedition, we sometimes dream of training. Really. We love it.

Did we do it for fame? No. To us, media attention is an annoying but necessary part of expedition fundraising and outreach for charity. We see many adventurers as self-promoters whose glorious failures are seized upon by the drama-addicted press and public relations agents. By contrast, some of the world's most successful explorers remain little-known.

We wanted a challenge that would push us beyond our perceived limits, one that would push us to higher levels of self-reliance and optimism. So we chose the granddaddy of polar challenges: an unsupported ski expedition to the North Pole. By the time we stepped onto the ice, only eleven separate expeditions—and no Americans—had accomplished this feat.

We are fascinated by the paradox of the unknown. It all boils down to fear and attraction. For us the attraction usually wins out. Venturing into the unknown gives us a feeling of exhilaration that is hard to describe, and hard to duplicate without returning there once again. We find it curiously addictive.

Since high school, Tyler and I have followed our passions rather than one of the standard paths that society lays out. It has always felt right to go after what we love—wilderness expeditions and experiential education—and pursue that instead.

We sometimes answer the question "Why?" by turning it around. Why does anyone do what they do? It's probably a combination of life choices, interests, and opportunities. In our case, we followed our hearts. Then we took it to another level. How about you? What if you could take your most prized skills and passions and apply them to a far-flung, mind-blowing, sometimes scary dream? What would you do? For us the North Pole was that dream, and we went for it.

But it was never just about the North Pole. It was always about the whole journey. We wanted the all-encompassing polar experience: the commitment, the planning, the fundraising, the training, the logistics, the emotions, the laughs and disagreements, the tasks and tedium, the failures and successes . . . and the Pole itself. How we did it was more important than just doing it. We wanted to do it with integrity and style. We wanted it all—the good, the bad, and the ugly. In the end, we got more than we could have imagined.

"No one can cheat you out of ultimate success but yourself." —Ralph Waldo Emerson

We define the term "unsupported" as follows: to travel using only human muscle power without outside assistance in the form of resupplies, medical aid, or food drops.

Tyler and I consider walking, running, paddling, and bicycling to be unsupported means of travel. In the polar expedition world, skiing and walking (mostly on snowshoes) are the unsupported means of travel. No sled dogs. No snowmobiles. At no time on an unsupported expedition can team members use anything other than what they've carried from the start, or what they find naturally occurring along the way. An unsupported expedition allows no second chances. It places a great deal of importance on preparation and resourcefulness. If something breaks, we have to fix it or do without.

A few years ago some members of the expedition community re-categorized expeditions by distinguishing between those that are "unsupported" and those that are "unassisted." The former refers to the use of human muscle power alone; the latter refers to traveling without resupplies or direct medical aid. Our definition covers all of the above.

Tyler and I have always believed in the adage, "Less is more." An unsupported trip is the expeditionary embodiment of this concept. It's only us and the elements. No matter what happens along the way, we have to deal with it and keep going. If we succeed, we own every bit of the success. If we fail, the responsibility is ours. No excuses. No second chances. For us an unsupported expedition is as pure as it gets—simple, honest, and transparent.

3 ARE YOU A YAHOO?

BY JOHN HUSTON

"Adventure is just bad planning." —Roald Amundsen

On a warm night in August of 2006, I stood on a deck overlooking the city of Oslo, Norway, with Rune Gjeldnes and his friend, Bjørn Loe. We chatted as we gazed out over the city lights and the fjord below. A few days earlier I'd told Rune of my plan to ski unsupported to the North Pole.

His response was, "I know you are the American to do it!" Right away he threw his full support behind the idea.

Later, on Bjørn's deck, we discussed sponsorship. Rune looked at me with his familiar intensity. "That will be the hardest part of the North Pole for you—raising the money."

I often thought about his words over the next two and a half years as we struggled to fund the expedition. Rune was right in many ways. Tyler and I had some of our greatest difficulties during the three years leading up to our time on the ice. Raising money wasn't the only obstacle, though. At times, personal issues between Tyler and me called our partnership into question.

In the fall of 2006, we got off to a strong start by crafting a mission statement to guide our marketing, outreach, and decision-making. On a sunny weekday afternoon in Tyler's dining room in Ely, over a lunch of smoked lake trout and Tyler's homemade bread, we came up with this statement:

Our mission is to use ambitious wilderness expeditions to inspire people to approach the challenges of life with optimism, humility, and responsibility.

We then defined our values:

Optimism: The unwavering belief in the positive potentials inherent in oneself, others, and society—an absolute commitment to positive outcomes.

Humility: The pragmatic ability to adapt to and learn from situations and other people, the defining characteristic of an unpretentious and modest person.

Responsibility: Acting with strong consideration for the environmental, social, and interpersonal impacts of one's actions.

It's safe to say that if we hadn't begun with a mission statement and a solid set of values, our partnership would have collapsed. Our plan was for me to spearhead fundraising and networking. Tyler would devote ten hours a week to the project while working full time at Outward Bound.

Determined to learn every nuance of Arctic Ocean travel, we set out on a quest for knowledge. We wanted to create our own "margin of success," our term for a deliberate attention to detail and preparation that would increase the likelihood of success and make it easier to absorb setbacks along the way.

Our role model was Roald Amundsen, a genius of planning and innovation. Amundsen's relentless drive to educate himself and his team set him apart from other explorers. Time and time again, he went out of his way to learn from the masters of specific crafts. He never stopped searching for improvements. Amundsen wasn't committed to a specific way of doing something—he was committed to finding the best way.

Unlike Amundsen, we could rely on a modern catalog of Arctic Ocean experience. Tyler and I pored over books and websites covering successful North Pole expeditions from the previous fifteen years. We took it one step further by setting up meetings with several modern pioneers we didn't already know. In Oslo I met with Børge Ousland, who suggested that we pull two small sleds instead of one large one and train for the expedition by dragging truck tires over dry land.

In the spring of 2007 I traveled to Ontario, Canada, to visit Richard Weber, who at that time had skied from land to the North Pole six separate times, beginning in 1986. In 1995 he and Russian Misha Malakhov completed an epic unsupported trip from Canada to the North Pole and back. Richard and his wife Josée design their own polar clothing and expedition equipment. I was hoping they'd sell me one of their custom-made polar tents. And I was hoping to pick their brains.

Richard and Josée had been Nordic skiers on the Canadian national team. When I arrived at their home in the wooded hills north of Ottawa, I sensed a strong-willed intensity in both of them. We had a beer on their deck and chatted about Ely and the American Birkebeiner. Then Josée took over.

"So, why are you here? You want to go the North Pole, do you?"

"Yes, unsupported," I said.

"Well. That's no walk in the park."

"I know. That's why I'm here," I said. "I'm interested in your tent."

"The tent! I'm never going to sew another one of those tents in my life. That's a lot of work. We've considered contracting out the sewing, but it's tricky. The

Josée Auclair. Former Canadian national team skier and veteran polar traveler.

stitching is the most important part."

Josée's stern, questioning look had never left her face.

"So, John, tell me," she continued. "Are you a yahoo?"

I took a sip of beer, wondering where this was going.

"We get a lot of yahoos coming here. You know, people who want to go to the North Pole who have never skied in their lives. Who just want some cheap headlines. Who don't know how to handle the cold and don't take the dangers seriously. We find such people disrespectful. They're a liability to work with." She peered at me. "We don't help just anyone who comes knocking.

"So, I want to know. Are you a yahoo?" Since getting to know the Webers I've come to think fondly of her blunt manner, but at the time it caused me to backpedal a bit.

"No. I'm not." I went into a description of our background and approach.

"Humble, you say. That's nice to hear." Josée softened her tone slightly. "You know that expeditions on Antarctica and Greenland are like holidays compared to the Arctic Ocean?"

Nodding, I began to outline our preparation schedule. I told her we were optimistic about funding.

"Oh, the fundraising. That was Richard's big challenge. But you let us know. If you get the money, then we'll see about the tent."

Richard remained silent throughout our exchange, but he seemed to project a supportive vibe. Finally, he said, "I have a good feeling about you guys. You're skiers. That means a lot. I have to put a lot of my clients on snowshoes because they can't ski. Snowshoeing is a bit slower and uses more energy, but it's more efficient for someone who can't ski."

I agreed, and we launched into a conversation about the hard-earned skill of skiing in soft boots with no ankle support. The talk wound from one polar topic to another and led into an evening of storytelling.

Later that year, during the summer of 2007, I found myself chasing down the millions of details required to pitch our expedition. Since I had time off between polar gigs, I was able to focus on the project. Tyler, who was overcommitted at work, struggled to contribute. I missed our brainstorming sessions, and I sometimes felt like I was crumbling under the pressure to raise $200,000.

In 2007, we couldn't afford to hire anyone to help with the project, and I drained my savings to get it off the ground. I took on the networking, website design, search for funding and equipment, educational and charity partnerships, and public relations.

I wracked my brain for companies that might sponsor us. Fortunately, Rune's strong ties with the outdoor company Bergans of Norway gave us a solid start. Bergans makes some of the best polar-specific clothing on the planet. In August I met with their North American director, who told me he'd be

Office effort. Too much time staring at the screen, but that's part of the whole package.

Richard Weber, polar legend. Seven trips on foot from land to the North Pole, most recently in 2010.

happy to supply us with clothing and equipment, and possibly funding. Tyler and I were thrilled, but that was a lone high point.

In early February 2008, when I returned home exhausted from the South Pole, my confidence in our partnership hit bottom.

We talked it through. Tyler told me that his other commitments had distracted him from advancing our project and that at times he lacked motivation. He also said that I was too much of a perfectionist and too critical of his efforts. He didn't feel empowered to make decisions on his own. I countered that I wanted to create a strong first impression with sponsors in a hypercompetitive arena.

Despite these conflicts, our communication remained honest and forward-thinking. I accepted the fact that Tyler was over-programmed and would continue to be. We agreed that I should take on the administrative tasks, while he focused on expedition research and planning.

In March of 2008 we flew to Iqaluit on Baffin Island, in Canada's Nunavut Territory, for a training expedition. On the way to Iqaluit we stopped in Ottawa for a two-day session with Richard Weber. This amounted to downloading volumes of thoroughly refined insights on diet, scheduling, ice drift, weather, gear, navigation, and countless other details from Richard's computer-like brain. Meeting with Richard was one of the best investments we could've made. Later that year we had similar sessions with Rune Gjeldnes and Sjur Mørdre.

Like Amundsen, we saw ourselves as synthesizers building upon the best knowledge available. Becoming friends with some of today's polar legends was one of the most satisfying and fun aspects of the entire journey.

We moved on to Iqaluit. During my stay in 2007, I had come to know the town's quirky vibe and made several friends. This time around we stayed with Matty McNair.

Located on the chilly shores of Frobisher Bay, Matty's home is a hive of activity. It's the perfect place for staging an Arctic expedition, with a fully outfitted workshop and plenty of space for storing and drying equipment. Matty herself is a wiry, red-haired dynamo, a natural teacher who never tires of sharing her knowledge. Like most polar veterans, she is opinionated and passionate about her craft.

Tyler and I set out on our training trip, ten days of skiing and snowshoeing. Our aim was to test equipment, routines, and travel methods and to put our bodies through the wringer. We loaded four plastic sleds with food, fuel, equipment, and enough sacks of dog food from Matty's sled dog yard to total 375 pounds per person. At a relatively balmy daytime temperature of 0° F, our sleds would slide easily. We added the extra weight to mimic the sand-like snow conditions of -40° F.

As we meandered over the hummocked ice, we sometimes chose the path of least resistance to simulate

Courtesy of Matty McNair

Matty McNair, polar dynamo.

the process of route-finding on the Arctic Ocean. At other times we chose the most difficult path in order to practice going through rubble. We hoisted our sleds by hand over pressure ridges on the sea ice and pulled them up through passes in the nearby hills.

We needed this time together. During the past two years Tyler and I had rarely been in the same place. On the first night we camped a few bays to the west of Iqaluit, beyond the glow of the town. The northern lights, arching in green curtains, shimmered in the sky above us. It was only 8:00 p.m., but we were ready for bed. We felt satisfied from a good day of skiing and a fatty pemmican dinner, and wondered why our lives at home couldn't be this simple.

Two days later we rendezvoused with Matty near a section of open water where she was instructing a polar training group. There, we practiced swimming open leads while wearing our waterproof drysuits. For polar explorers, the drysuit is an indispensable piece of safety equipment. If you fall through the ice

Dog yard bay. Matty McNair's team of sled dogs and a slice of Iqaluit's shoreline.

Frozen beach. View from Matty's house, looking out onto Frobisher Bay.

Rubble coast. Training on Frobisher Bay. Tyler coaxes his way through.

If training's not tough, it's not training. John works through the maze with 370 pounds behind him.

without one, your life is in danger. In a drysuit you can stay safe and in control of the situation.

The swimming exercise was more fun than expected, and strangely relaxing. With that behind us, we set off on our own again.

So far the weather had been mild. Thankfully, we soon ran into high winds and a near whiteout, which allowed us to do some real testing. The wind threatened to knock us off our feet. We skied along deliberately, careful to maintain contact with each other. Setting up camp was an ordeal. One careless move and the tent would be blown away.

We relished the challenge. Skiing through a whiteout near open water would be one of the riskiest scenarios we might face on our way to the Pole. Since we would have only fifty-five days to get there, we'd have to keep pushing during bad weather.

Heavy evening. Tyler hauls across Frobisher Bay.

Frobisher's 37-foot foot. John stares up at the ice foot of an island on Frobisher Bay. The ice he is standing on rises and descends more than thirty feet with the tides, hiding and revealing the ice foot.

Early spring dip. John tests the waters.

Polar swimsuit pose. Not quite the cover shot.

The storm broke two days later and we skied back to town, sweating under the hot sun. Hot for Iqaluit anyway.

It had been a solid trip. Working together felt good. Still, I was anxious about the next year. The expedition wasn't funded yet, and I dreaded returning to the loneliness and pressure of that Sisyphean search.

Later that spring, I sent emails to twenty gear companies pitching our expedition. I was hopeful because I thought our project was unique. At the same time, I steeled myself for rejection.

One night in May I sat in my apartment in Chicago, combing watch company websites for phone numbers. My emails had yielded promises of equipment, but no prospects of funding. Watch companies had helped fund many expeditions in the past, but the specter of cold calling was depressing. Without a personal contact, these companies seemed impregnable.

I didn't like working alone and my bank account was screaming at me. Optimism was one of our values, but that evening I wasn't feeling it—$200,000 seemed out of reach. We were scheduled to hit the ice in nine months.

The next morning, as I revamped our website for the third time since 2006, providence finally shined.

Twice.

First, I got a call from DeLorme, publisher of the well-known topographical state atlases. They had recently introduced the GPS unit I carried to the South Pole. Their marketing manager invited me to come to their headquarters in Maine to discuss sponsorship. I immediately phoned Tyler with the good news.

Two hours later, I received an enthusiastic email from a sales director at Victorinox Swiss Army, the legendary manufacturer of Swiss Army Knives. He asked me to visit Victorinox's North American headquarters in Connecticut. I whooped, called Tyler again and tried to temper my enthusiasm, knowing that nothing was definite.

For months I'd felt a strong premonition that these two companies would come through. Their values aligned perfectly with ours, so a partnership seemed natural. I booked a flight and got to work refining my presentations.

I was nervous going in, but both meetings went perfectly. After a few months of hammering out the contracts, Victorinox Swiss Army became the official knife sponsor, timepiece sponsor, and expedition title sponsor, hence the project's name: the Victorinox North Pole '09 Expedition. DeLorme signed on as our official GPS

Happy campers. Training expedition complete, less than a year till the big one.

Courtesy of Jim Paulson

sponsor. Bergans of Norway came on board in the fall as our official performance apparel sponsor. Contributions from personal donors were rolling in. For the first time, our finances were in great shape. After months of doubt, it looked like the trip might actually happen.

By John Huston

The history of North Pole exploration is shrouded in controversy. Today a fierce debate still rages over two competing century-old American claims. In 1906 both Frederick Cook and Robert Peary independently declared themselves to be the first to reach the North Pole. Cook claimed to have reached it in 1905, during the previous expedition season. Each called the other a liar, and neither claim has stood the test of time. Some researchers believe that Cook fabricated photographs and likely never ventured more than one hundred miles north of land. Peary's navigation records and stated pace of travel have been called into question. The fact that both men carried unsavory reputations only bolsters these doubts.

Tyler and I find most aspects of the Cook and Peary saga thoroughly uninspiring. Peary, for example, is said to have had a penchant for acting as a bystander while his unheralded Inuit team built igloos, drove the dogs, and maneuvered the sleds. In our opinion, whether either one of them made it simply doesn't matter at this point.

The first documented expedition to the North Pole took place in 1926 when the airship *Norge*, manned by Roald Amundsen, Umberto Nobile,

Robert E. Peary.

and fourteen others, flew over 90° N. It wasn't until 1968 that Minnesotan Ralph Plaisted and three companions completed the first confirmed surface expedition to the North Pole—via snowmobile with resupplies. The next year Wally Herbert of Britain and three teammates dogsledded to the North Pole on their way to completing a monumental crossing of the Arctic Ocean from Alaska to Svalbard, Norway. Herbert's expedition began in February 1968 and ended in May 1969, receiving several resupplies along the way. In 1986 Will Steger and Paul Schurke of Ely, Minnesota, led the first confirmed unresupplied expedition to the North Pole. In 1990 Norwegians Børge Ousland and Erling Kagge completed the first unsupported expedition to the North Pole. Four years later Børge became the first to do it solo and unsupported.

One hundred years ago, before airplanes existed, polar explorers were faced with an expedition twice as long as ours: from land to the North Pole and back. Today only two expeditions have completed that trip unsupported. In 1995 Canadian Richard Weber (a member of Steger and Schurke's 1986 team) and Russian Misha Malakhov skied from Canada to the North Pole and back to Canada in 108 days. In 2000 Norwegians Rune Gjeldnes and Torry Larsen skied from Russia to the North Pole to Canada in 109 days. In our minds these are the most impressive North Pole expeditions ever accomplished. However, due largely to the modesty of these men, neither expedition received much notoriety.

Courtesy of the Fram Museum, Oslo

Norge, **Amundsen and Nobile's airship, 1926.**

Frederick Cook.

CLAIMS ON THE POLE

Date	Name	Flag	Method	Notes
April 22, 1908	Frederick Cook	🇺🇸	Dogsled	
April 6, 1909	Robert Peary	🇺🇸	Dogsled	
May 12, 1926	Roald Amundsen and Umberto Nobile		Airship	
April 19, 1968	Ralph Plaisted	🇺🇸	Snowmobiles	Resupplied
April 6, 1969	Wally Herbert		Dogsled	Arctic Ocean crossing, resupplied
May 1, 1986	Will Steger and Paul Schurke		Dogsled	Unresupplied
May 4, 1990	Børge Ousland and Erling Kagge		Skis	Unsupported
April 23, 1994	Børge Ousland		Skis	Solo, unsupported
June 15, 1995	Richard Weber and Misha Malakhov		Skis	Round trip, unsupported
June 25, 2000	Rune Gjeldnes and Torry Larsen		Skis	Arctic Ocean crossing, unsupported

Paul Schurke and Will Steger.

Courtesy of Paul Schurke and Will Steger

Børge Ousland and Erling Kagge.

Courtesy of Børge Ousland

Richard Weber and Misha Malakhov.

Courtesy of Richard Weber

Rune Gjeldnes and Torry Larsen.

Courtesy of Rune Gjeldnes

BY JOHN HUSTON

Piotr Bednarski.

Courtesy of Piotr Bednarski

Morning donuts.
John builds up
some torque.

I like to say that training is the expedition. How well we prepared our minds and bodies in advance would determine our chances of success.

In one sense, our physical training really was the expedition, because without it we would have failed miserably. In another sense, our training was the expedition broken down into smaller components, but taking place in familiar surroundings—our hometowns of Chicago and Ely.

Our regimen was designed to build muscle and establish muscle memory by simulating the motions of skiing to the North Pole. We would need enough strength, stamina, and technical skill to haul our three-hundred-pound sleds for fifty-five days across vast stretches of amazingly variable ice and snow, heave them by hand through sprawling junkyards of ice rubble, and then endure an all-out sprint to the finish. Injury prevention would be an absolute key to reaching the Pole. We split our preparation for these challenges into five categories: endurance training, strength training, mental training, flexibility, and weight gain.

With backgrounds in cross-country ski racing, Tyler and I had already built a good base of endurance. We both had a big appetite for long hours in the sun and the weight room. And perhaps most importantly we were also hungry for advice. Børge Ousland, a Norwegian polar pioneer, recommended pulling tires while walking with ski poles to simulate pulling the sleds. We hired Piotr Bednarski from Minneapolis, Minnesota, to design our training routines and schedule. He's an accomplished cross-country ski racer, trainer, and coach, and the Athlete Development Director for the U.S. Biathlon Team. Piotr's expertise was invaluable. By following his workouts we made major gains right away, which further pumped up our motivation.

In the spring of 2007, Tyler and I started our training program:

Courtesy of Matthew Taplinger, nonformat.org

Chicago shore. John pulls tires on North Avenue Beach.

ENDURANCE TRAINING consisted of hooking myself up to two pickup truck tires and hauling them behind me with the aid of ski poles for two to five hours at a stretch. The tires weighed only forty-five pounds each, but it was friction that determined the intensity of the workout. Pulling them over grass or clean concrete created the most friction. Pulling them through the city of Chicago elicited all sorts of stares and comments from passersby. Sometimes my presence actually slowed traffic. Most of the comments were related to cars or punishment. My favorites: "What did you do to your wife?" "Isn't it easier to roll them?" "Are you being punished for something?" "Can I ride in those?" "I hope you didn't steal those off my car." And of course, "Dude, where's your car?!?"

STRENGTH TRAINING took place in the gym and outdoors. The goal was to develop strong, resilient core muscles—crucial for preventing injuries. Our gym routines were centered around sixteen different free-weight exercises, all designed to work multiple joints and improve

Canadian chow-down.
The boys go to work on some Tim Horton's breakfast sandwiches, Ottawa.

Tyler in the gym.

© David J. Owen

balance. We loved hitting the gym and busting out those routines at 5:30 a.m., before starting our workdays. We also trained for strength by pulling heavy tires in quick bursts over very short distances. I dragged five pickup tires at a time for these workouts, while Tyler hitched himself to a 200-pound tractor tire.

FLEXIBILITY TRAINING included extra attention to stretching after workouts.

MENTAL TRAINING took many different forms. Our physical training plan, especially the long periods of tire pulling and the discipline needed to follow the schedule, mimicked the pace and structure of expedition travel. Over time we were able to relax and feel comfortable with the drudgery, tedium, and mental fatigue of training. This gave us confidence. We put our bodies through the wringer, knowing that the real expedition would do the same. Often while hauling tires we practiced positive visualization by imagining on-ice scenarios in which we solved problems, and by envisioning the hard work required to succeed.

WEIGHT GAIN prior to hitting the ice is essential. On a long polar expedition a person simply can't ingest enough calories to meet the energy requirements of exertion in deep-freeze temperatures. When fuel from the digestive system runs out, the body first grabs calories from its fat stores, and when the fat is depleted, from the muscles. To forestall this last eventuality, Tyler and I bulked up twenty pounds beyond our normal body weights. This is not as easy or as fun as one might think. I've found the simplest way to maintain extra weight when training is to add a heavy portion of butter to every meal. About six weeks before leaving for the Pole, we began a period of no-holds-barred food consumption, which luckily coincided with the winter holidays. We kept fatty foods close by all day long and crammed in as many calories as we could. It's fun to do this when you're hungry, but we began to feel gross and bloated as our bodies added a layer of fat on top of our hard-earned muscles.

41

BY JOHN HUSTON   JANUARY 21–MARCH 2, 2009

"Getting out the door is just damn stressful! It's the nature of the beast. For an unsupported expedition,

the pressure to get it right before hitting the ice is huge." —Matty McNair, February 23, 2009

It's hard to describe what it takes to launch an expedition. It's as if you're pulling on a freight train, trying to get it rolling. Once the train leaves the station, you're on it till the end of the line. But before it leaves, you feel increasingly pinched by the manifold stresses of final preparation and departure. All the while, the deadline looms.

During the last week of January 2009, Tyler and a few friends from Outward Bound packed our expedition gear into fifteen duffle bags. Some items were late in arriving from Norway and Canada, which forced us to pack alternates in case the shipments didn't make it. This would mean more last-minute tinkering. As much as we'd planned otherwise, these nagging complications wouldn't stop until we hit the ice.

Tyler spent his last days with Ethan and Sarah at his boyhood home, thirty miles north of Minneapolis. He enjoyed his parents' home cooking, but spent much of the time running errands and tying up loose ends. He barely slept.

Expedition charm. Sarah, Tyler's wife, presents him with her lucky polar bear necklace.

A sense of foreboding loomed as events drew him toward a wrenching farewell. He'd be leaving his wife and five-month-old son. He might also be saying a final goodbye to Bud, his creaky old German Shepherd.

On the morning of February 8, just before heading to the airport, Sarah tied a small necklace around Tyler's neck. From the cord hung a little silver polar bear. This was the same necklace he had given her to wear on her expedition across the Canadian Arctic in 2004.

Later that day my girlfriend Jennifer and I met my parents at O'Hare Airport in Chicago. Once in a while I get these big premonitions about life, and one of those times was when I met Jennifer through friends seven months earlier. She was an attorney who'd been raised in a small town outside of Chicago. When we first spent time together I was bowled over. Pretty soon it was obvious that we shared a powerful connection. I thought she was gorgeous, and I admired the grounded and thoughtful way she went about things. Somehow I just knew we would get married.

We began dating in mid-November, just two and a half months before I was scheduled to leave for Canada. During that stretch we fell in love, celebrated the holidays, attended my sister's wedding, and started planning our life together. At the same time I was buzzing around getting the expedition ready to launch. She identified with my quest and never once asked "Why?" In our final days together we ate at our favorite ethnic restaurants in Chicago—Japanese, Mexican, Italian, and Thai. These dinners created some vivid sense memories to call up during the long days on the ice.

Tyler joined us at O'Hare. He and I looked like dorky twins. By accident we were both wearing jeans and identical green Bergans T-shirts. My parents had brought lunch from my favorite taqueria, and we all sat on a bench in the terminal, stuffing our faces with guacamole and bean burritos.

To build fat reserves we'd been binge-eating since Thanksgiving and it showed. Both of us were at least twenty pounds heavier than normal. I tipped the scales at more than 190 pounds and Tyler was well over 200.

Tears at parting. Tyler and Sarah in their final moments before departure.

Emotions overflowed as I said goodbye. The moment felt surreal. I hugged my parents. My mother burst into tears and pleaded with me to be safe. Jennifer and I held each other. Through watery eyes she smiled and told me she would be all right. "I'll see you in Norway," she said. I watched her as she walked out of the terminal. Then I proceeded to our gate.

Tyler and I had met our deadline. We felt good about that, but we'd failed to avoid all the associated stresses. In the beginning we talked about not letting the interviews, blog entries, school presentations, and administrivia get in the way of preparation. Instead, the endless to-do list had overwhelmed us. Our mistake was waiting too long to hire our expedition manager, Kristin Daniels. We should have had her on board months earlier. I'll never forget scurrying around Chicago trying to find a place to freeze-dry eighty pounds of cheddar cheese after learning it wouldn't be waiting in Ottawa.

We were leaving three weeks early to escape the distractions of home. With the anxiety of our goodbyes behind us, we settled in for some quiet time on the plane.

Pudgy on purpose. Twins by accident. Jennifer can't believe it.

Bacon below zero. Outside Matty McNair's house in Iqaluit, John fries up all the bacon for the expedition.

Cheese man. John packages the freeze-dried cheese.

The flight to Ottawa was one big sigh of relief. Three more flights before we hit the ice. Each one would narrow our focus.

We stopped at Richard Weber's house near Ottawa to pick up the tent we'd ordered ten months earlier, along with 150 pounds of pemmican and chocolate truffles. Richard had some bad news. The tent wasn't ready. He promised to ship it to Iqaluit the following week, but we were bummed. Another complication.

That evening we shared venison, artisan cheese, homemade bread, and other delicacies with Richard, Josée, and their two sons. Memories of this hearty spread would stick with us throughout the expedition. Tyler and I chatted with Richard about sled weights, fuel usage, snow conditions, and drift.

"I'm impressed with your planning," he told us. "I think you guys can make it."

In order to take advantage of the weak Canadian dollar, we planned to procure some of our supplies in Canada. The next day we checked out of a supermarket, our cart overflowing with 150 packages of ramen noodles and thirty pounds of butter.

That was fun, but the strain of leaving home had ebbed only slightly. Tyler was driving all over Ottawa picking up the last bits and pieces of expedition kit. I was still tethered to my computer, staying up late editing and uploading videos for our sponsors. Worst of all, my ski boots had yet to be shipped from Norway, even though I ordered them four months earlier, way back in November.

The lack of sleep and hectic pace were taking their toll. Several times Tyler and I butted heads, taking our stress out on each other. We could have eased the burden by hiring someone to travel with us and help out. Again we realized this too late. It was all on us.

I remembered Rune saying to me, "It's a good idea you have, to prepare in Iqaluit for two weeks. But you won't stop dealing with distractions until your plane lands on the ice!"

On February 12 we deplaned at Iqaluit into the teeth of a roaring snowstorm. The Arctic cold ripped into our skin as we loaded up Matty's battered blue minivan. We had packed our mittens deep in a duffle bag, so we grabbed some wool socks and pulled them onto our hands.

Over the next few days we took over Matty's workshop, sewing room, and storage sheds. We packed all of our food into five-day rations and went to work making our equipment expedition-ready. Except for the tent and my boots, we

Polar workshop. John modifies a heat exchanger (which increases stove efficiency).

finally had all of our equipment in one place. In the evenings we continued to train by hauling Matty's unwieldy pulks—loaded with four hundred pounds of sled dog food—over the broken ice of Frobisher Bay.

Twelve days in Iqaluit would allow our bodies to acclimate. With prolonged exposure to the cold, the body increases circulation, which prevents the extremities from getting cold as easily. This is something we both had experienced for some time. By the end of most of our winters in Ely, Tyler and I had adapted so well that at 30° F we just wore a thin shirt. Some North Pole seekers don't acclimatize properly and end up quitting after a few days on the ice. To our dismay, the temperature on our evening jaunts through the rubble hovered around a balmy 0° F. We sweated like crazy.

One evening our Inuit friend Meeka Mike invited us to her home to celebrate the birthday of Livee Kululluik, an Inuit elder, ace hunter, nonstop comedian, and Popeye-armed wilderness tough guy. Livee, Meeka, and I had traveled a few hundred miles together by snowmobile in 2007. Although he speaks little English,

Meeka Mike.

Livee Kululluik.

Cold Hawker. Our Hawker Siddeley 748.

Livee joked with us all evening, laughing with his big, mostly toothless grin. The feast included seal meat, fresh turbot, and big biscuits called bannock. Livee's lighthearted outlook served as a poignant reminder for Tyler and me. The hard times would be a lot easier if we held onto our sense of humor.

Meanwhile, Tyler had caught a nasty bug. He was coughing and looked run-down. He kept saying he didn't feel as bad has he looked and never complained, but I really felt for him. We were getting along pretty well now but still had our moments of sniping, mostly about what to do next and how to get it done. We weren't having as much fun as Livee.

But our work ethic never flagged. We mounted our sled runners and added long leashes to jacket zippers and just about everything else we'd have to handle with our mittens on. We made countless adjustments to increase efficiency, like mounting our stoves on a metal board so we wouldn't have to set them up each night. These vital steps increased our sense of control. However, we couldn't control everything. My boots still hadn't shown up.

I used the same model of boot—the Alfa Mørdre Pro—in Greenland and Antarctica for over 2,100 miles and got just one tiny blister. Foot health was a huge priority. We obsessed over it. Tyler and I had put a lot of time and effort into testing another boot and binding system, but neither of us liked it as much as the simple, reliable Norwegian three-pin, coupled with the Alfas. Our plane was scheduled to leave for Resolute in forty-eight hours. The prospect of switching to our second choice was more than a little unsettling.

Gourmet grub. Testing out the pemmican stew. Fat like this shouldn't be consumed indoors.

On top of that, the saga of our tent took a sharp turn for the worse. Richard called to say that the new tent had arrived. But it was the wrong size! By mistake the factory had made a four-person tent. Bigger was not better. It would be twice as heavy and a lot colder, due to unfilled space. I hung up the phone and let loose a stream of curses.

Richard called back later and offered us the same tent we had used for training on Baffin the previous year. (He had already taken this tent to the North Pole in 2006.) We wanted to accept his offer, but doubted the reliability of the seams. We would put off a final decision until we had it in our hands. There was another problem. Could Richard find a way to send it to Resolute? He would have to find a person traveling there from Ottawa who was willing to bring it along.

Just before we left Iqaluit for Resolute, my boots arrived. They fit perfectly—at least my feet would be happy.

On February 25, we flew to Resolute. As our lives simplified with each flight north, the size of the plane decreased accordingly. Our Hawker Siddeley 748 looked like it had seen a few too many Arctic winters. The cabin featured a bucket for a toilet and less than a dozen seats. It wasn't pressurized, but it was plenty warm. We could've fried bacon on the heating ducts at our feet.

We flew north into a deep twilight, where the sun had recently risen for the first time in months. After years of planning, we were finally setting forth into the unknown.

Landing in total darkness, we entered the wonderful lunacy of an outpost of civilization known as Resolute, population 229. The town sits huddled at the base of a huge bluff. In the winter every unshoveled space is mounded high with snow.

Aziz Kheraj met us on the runway in a fifteen-person van. Aziz is a balding man from Tanzania who married a local Inuit woman. He operates the South

Airport twilight. Hall Beach Airport, where our plane refueled en route to Resolute.

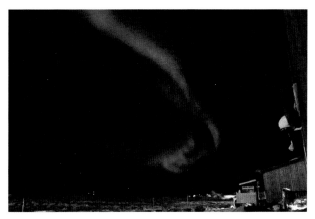
Iqaluit night lights.

Surreal arrival. Deplaning in Resolute on February 25.

Camp Inn, a build-out of an old Canadian military barracks. The sprawling inn, its exterior a weather-blasted mix of flaking yellow paint and naked particleboard, dominates the southeastern corner of town.

We crashed into bed at 1:00 a.m. on February 26. If the weather cooperated, we'd be on a plane headed for Ward Hunt Island in just over seventy-two hours.

The next day, for the first time, we weighed our loaded sleds—two that measured sixty-three inches long and two that measured fifty-one. Cargo flight schedules had prevented us from doing this until now. Aziz's scale told us we'd each

Sprawling abode. The South Camp Inn, Resolute.

John and Aziz.

Food sled. Tyler arranges the contents of his big sled. His sleeping pad is adorned with drawings and words of support from friends.

be hauling 330 pounds. Fifty pounds more than we'd hoped for! The extra weight would kill our pace.

We decided to cut weight by reducing our food supply for the first half of the trip. We split the food into three stages: 5,700 calories per day for the first two weeks, 6,700 for the next two weeks, and up to 7,500 for the final four weeks. We knew our appetites would increase as the trip progressed. We were happy with the solution, but it required us to repack and reweigh a month's worth of food. The next day the sleds weighed in at three hundred pounds per person. We decided to go with that.

Tyler was really feeling the lack of sleep, which didn't help his cold. We couldn't wait to get on the ice, if only for a few long, uninterrupted nights of sleep.

Those few days in Resolute were some of the most trying of the entire project. The stress wore us down and frayed our nerves. And we still weren't free of the administrative tentacles. Again, we paid dearly for not bringing along an assistant. We managed to stay on top of everything, but it felt like our minds were in a vise.

Late in the evening of February 27, Lonnie Dupre arrived in Resolute with our tent. A fellow Minnesotan, Lonnie was guiding a resupplied expedition to the Pole. He'd rendezvoused with Richard Weber in Ottawa. There was a chance we would bump into Lonnie later on the ice.

We set up the tent immediately and climbed in. It felt like home. A thorough check of the seams revealed only a few tiny holes. We emailed photos to Richard, and Tyler, who is a pro at little fix-it jobs, set to work reinforcing potential weak spots.

We called Richard for feedback. He reminded us that in 1995 he had used an identical tent for 108 days on the Arctic Ocean, with no signs of failure. After talking it over, Tyler and I decided to go for it. We laughed that it deserved a chance to be the only tent in the world to reach the North Pole unsupported twice.

The next day we loaded our gear into the De Havilland Twin Otter that was scheduled to fly us to Ward Hunt Island the following morning. Joining us were Christina Franco, who was attempting to become the first woman to ski solo to the North Pole, and her expedition manager, Jason De Carteret. The four of us had shared the big preparation room at South Camp Inn. It was fun trading jokes and comparing notes on what lay ahead.

That evening we learned that a large cloud system over northern Ellesmere Island would delay the flight by at least one day. Except for a few hours of murky

Yard sale. We take over the big meeting room at the South Camp Inn.

Air Otter. De Havilland Twin Otter in the hangar at Resolute Airport.

Tyler tinkering. Wiring the stoves to the stove board. From left: compass belt, stove bottle, tent brush, thermometer, tent pegs, and first-aid kit.

Pocket stitch. Tyler modifies the pockets on his jacket. A stuffed wolf looks on.

twilight, that area was still shrouded by the polar darkness. Our pilot was an Arctic Ocean veteran, and he was taking no chances. We lost a day of travel but welcomed the chance for some rest.

We spent the next day—the first of March—tying up loose ends. I retested our HP iPaq, the small PDA we would use to send photos and emails via our satellite phone. Tyler made some more clothing modifications and took care of some details on the home front. We wrote letters to Sarah and Jennifer, and I struggled for a few hours to set up the audiobooks and music on my iPod. I was losing sleep

over this, but it was better to take care of it now in a warm hotel room than later in a -40° F tent.

The last minute details were eating us alive. We'd been operating on very little sleep. Tyler's cough persisted, and his eyes still looked puffy. To be starting the expedition run down and mentally exhausted wasn't exactly how we planned it. I went to bed that night with a knot in my gut.

Two hours later the phone rang. It was Aziz. The flight was a go. The van would be leaving in thirty minutes.

By John Huston

As full-length North Pole expeditions go, an unsupported trip from Canada is the least expensive, since there's no need for costly resupply flights and airdrops. That said, we spent about $60,000 (USD) on airfare alone.

It isn't easy to get from Chicago to Ward Hunt Island, the northernmost point in North America. Scheduled flights only go as far north as the Inuit town of Resolute (located on Cornwallis Island at 74° N, near the southern edge of Ellesmere Island). Ward Hunt lies just off the opposite end of Ellesmere, 633 miles north of Resolute. Fortunately, we saved a lot of money by splitting the cost of chartering a De Havilland Twin Otter from Resolute to Ward Hunt with Christina Franco, an Italian who was making a solo resupplied attempt at the Pole.

The Twin Otter is the classic workhorse of the Polar regions—and anywhere else on Earth that requires a rugged, versatile airplane. Powered by twin turbine

Airport puzzle. John prepares for baggage check-in, Ottawa. Fifteen pieces of luggage!

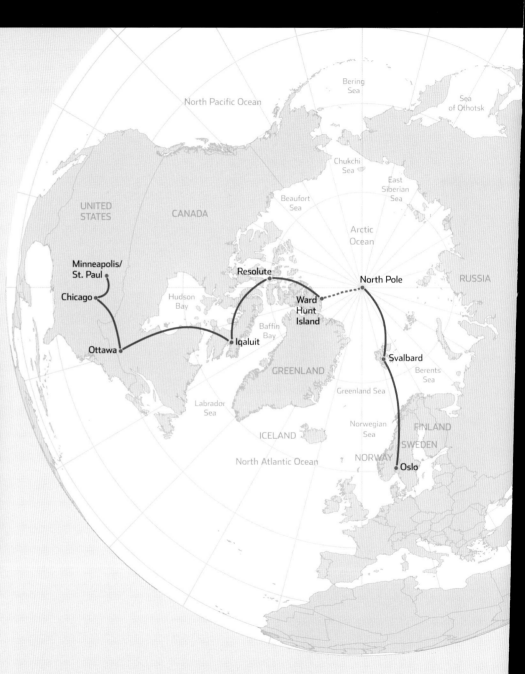

Polar plane. De Havilland Twin Otter, Antarctica.

Big Russian dragonfly. MI-8 helicopter near the North Pole.

engines, it can land on snow using skis, on water using pontoons, and on a variety of other surfaces using wheels. It requires only a little more than the length of a football field to take off and land. The no-frills fuselage can hold up to sixteen people or a payload of up to 1,400 pounds with full fuel tanks. Most Twin Otters flying today were built in the 1960s and 1970s and have been completely rebuilt several times over.

We contracted with a Russian polar logistics company to be picked up at the end of our journey. During the month of April each year, this company operates Barneo, a temporary airstrip located on the sea ice near the Pole. Barneo is the base camp for a swarm of researchers, journalists, adventure tourists, and expeditioners. The Russians use giant orange and blue MI-8 helicopters to shuttle people about the area.

Norway's Svalbard archipelago (at 78° N) is only a two-and-a-half-hour flight from Barneo. Once in Svalbard, clients reconnect to the conventional airline network for their flights back home. The total cost to fly us from the North Pole to Svalbard was $24,054.82.

During the first three months of 2009, $0.80 U.S. bought $1.00 Canadian. This favorable exchange rate saved us at least $10,000.

5 BLUES BEFORE SUNRISE

BY TYLER FISH

"One doesn't discover new lands without consenting to lose sight of the shore for a very long time." —André Gide

I climbed onto the plane in the predawn darkness and sat in the back behind John, Christina, and Jason. The seats up front had been removed to make space for our sleds, which were strapped down near the two-man cockpit.

The twin engines roared as plumes of snow swirled past my window. We were airborne in no time. As the plane banked north, I could see the lights of Resolute below. The town seemed to be hibernating. The roar settled into a deep, whirring drone that engulfed the small cabin. John turned around and gave me a thumbs-up. We were on our way.

For the next hour and a half I immersed myself in writing letters appreciating the most important people in my life: my parents for giving me the freedom to roam and find myself, my sister whose parenting I greatly respect, my Outward Bound colleagues for picking up my slack, and Ethan and Sarah, whom I love more than anything and who would be with me every day of the trip. I finished the last letter with tears

Back of the plane. Tyler's view. John plays with the GPS.

in my eyes. Launching this expedition had been tough on all of them. Leaving my wife and infant child behind was one of the hardest things I've ever done.

The dawn of a late Arctic winter revealed stunning views of Ellesmere Island. Mountains, glaciers, and sloping snowfields glowed in the pink light of the waking sun. I put my head back and relaxed.

Several hours later, we flew over the mountainous northern edge of Ellesmere Island, and there it was: the Arctic Ocean.

I was eager to get on the ice, but a part of me dreaded it. That's the beauty and tension of beginning. For now I was just glad to be done with all the preparations.

As the Twin Otter descended, we finally caught sight of the snow-covered cone that marks Ward Hunt Island, just off the north coast of Ellesmere. The plane was fitted with skis, which would allow us to land on flat snow at the base of the slope. Our pilot circled a

Ellesmere sunrise.

Noon twilight. Unloading the plane at 12:15 p.m., March 2.

Northernmost North America. Ward Hunt Island, the dome right under the wing. The frozen lead is in the foreground.

Got everything?

few times. Then he flew low to test the landing conditions, barely skimming the snow. Another circle and we touched down. The engines sputtered to a halt and two minutes later the pilots opened the doors.

We climbed down the ladder onto hard-packed snow. Together, we carefully unloaded the sleds. The pilots began walking the landing area, marking it with black garbage bags filled with snow.

It was time to look around. A perfect day: -40° F, clear and calm, with a crescent moon hanging in the evening-like sky. The rounded pyramid of Ward Hunt was right next to us, but what grabbed my attention were the coastal mountains of Ellesmere, poking their heads up from a sea of snowy glaciers. The rugged coast faded away toward Greenland far to the east.

As I slowly turned 360°, a seamless progression of colors emerged beyond the mountains where the sun lay hidden. A weak orange turned to pink, then light purple, on to a pastel blue, and then a deeper blue.

Jason and the pilots snapped some photos and offered words of encouragement. Then they clambered aboard and shut the doors. The roar assaulted our ears as the

Go time.

Goodbye, known world. Snow crystals stirred up by the takeoff hang in the air.

Down the ice shelf. John, with Christina Franco in the distance.

propellers stirred up little tornados of snow. Then the plane was up, dipping its wings and angling south. The sound of the engines ebbed and disappeared.

It was quiet. Christina hugged us goodbye and we wished her good luck. We tried to shoot some video, but the camera wouldn't focus in the cold. We were alone. Christina was now a distant dark figure against the white horizon.

John turned to me. "All set?"

"Yes."

"All right. Here we go." He said this with a hint of disbelief. Without further

ceremony, he skied away.

"Yup," I said to myself, "here we go." I took a deep breath. It was nagging me that something more should be said.

I waited to take that first step. Maybe I was enjoying the view. Maybe I wanted to get the photo of John and Christina skiing into the distance. Maybe I wanted to feel the enormous presence of the Arctic Ocean in front of me. With one big tug on the sleds, I left North America behind.

At the other end of this expedition was a helicopter ride from the North Pole to

Barneo, the temporary Russian base near the Pole. Since the Barneo base depended on good ice, the Russians had set a firm pullout date of April 26. On that day the helicopter would pick us up, wherever we happened to be, and transport us to Barneo. From there we would fly to Norway to meet our families.

For the first half-mile or so, as the ice shelf sloped down to the floating ice of the ocean, it almost felt like any other outing. Part of me wanted it to feel unique, skiing to the North Pole, but years of training and experience tempered that expectation. Even so, I couldn't help but smile.

I was settling into a nice rhythm when my left ski came off. It lay there on the snow in front of my pulk. I tried stepping into the binding again. But no matter how hard I pushed or how carefully I lined up the pins, I couldn't get the toe of my boot to fit securely into the binding. Could this really be happening?

My boot gaiter was getting in the way, causing the pins to press into the wrong part of the sole. We'd been forced to wait till the last minute to fit our Alfa boots with gaiters (insulating covers). As a result, I had glued them onto my boots and took them on the expedition without a good, thorough testing.

I strapped the skis to my large pulk and started walking. Better to make a closer inspection in the warmth of the tent than to keep skiing and potentially make things worse. I was mad at myself, but I couldn't worry about it now. We would be walking or snowshoeing through the rubble for the next few days anyway. I'd have plenty of time to fix the problem.

I caught up with John just before we reached the edge of the Ward Hunt Ice Shelf. A frozen lead marked the transition to the Ocean itself. John's hat and neck gaiter were covered with frost. Likewise, I could feel the stiff sensation of ice clinging to the stubble on my face.

After discussing my binding problem and the pending darkness, we decided to set up camp, stepping easily into our well-practiced routines. John moved with confidence—I could tell he was feeling good. We had finally entered expedition mode.

Inside the tent we turned on our headlamps and sat in peaceful silence for a minute.

John lit the stoves to melt snow. A few drops of

Polar sweat.

fuel had leaked out of one of our detachable stove pumps. The leak was tiny, but any amount was enough to make us wary. There was no sign of leakage for the rest of the evening. Like my troublesome ski binding, this was a puzzle we knew we could solve. Except for these concerns, and my lingering cough, the day had gone pretty well.

After dinner we joked around as we patiently went through the ten-minute process of wriggling into our sleeping bags and stowing our cold-sensitive belongings inside.

We slept for thirteen hours.

But that was okay. During the dark and cold of the first week we planned on sleeping long hours and traveling short, manageable days. This would relieve stress and give us time to focus on essentials. We didn't want to burn ourselves out.

The morning wasn't nearly as dark as we expected. We'd thought that navigating the jumbled ice would be complicated by darkness, but that wasn't the case. We could see fine without our headlamps. The dawn lasted more or less all day.

Our first steps went up and over the pressure ridge just beyond our tent. A pressure ridge is essentially a string of miniature ice mountains formed by colliding ice floes. Directly on the other side of the ridge sat a frozen lead that separated the Ward Hunt Ice Shelf from the Arctic Ocean. A six-inch crack filled with black seawater ran along the southern edge of the lead. The surface of the lead was speckled with frost flowers two inches high. We clambered down, stepped over the crack onto the frozen lead, and walked across.

We pulled one sled at a time through a field of ice blocks and little knolls that reminded me of Viking burial mounds. The snow creaked underfoot and our pulks groaned and screeched as we dragged them over the super cold ice and snow. These sounds, an indication of extreme friction, added to the sense that we were operating in an otherworldly realm. Occasionally, we'd climb one of the higher mounds looking for the path of least resistance through the jumble. Our scouting yielded spectacular views, but no obvious passage. I worried about finding a flat space large enough for the tent.

Down to the first lead.

Ice mountain. John scouts for a route.

Six hours later and only 0.87 nautical miles farther north, we stopped short of our intended time. We'd found a little spot for our tent that we dared not pass up.

Thirty minutes later, inside the tent, John fired up the twin MSR Whisperlite stoves. Warmth began to radiate. We sat there for a minute, savoring our first full travel day.

"Fire!" I shouted. Yellow flames raced beneath the stoves and onto the tent floor.

Our instincts took over. I yanked open the tent's double drawstring door. John grabbed the flaming stoveboard and tossed it outside. All was calm again. Outside the stoves hissed and steamed in the snow. Inside the air smelled of burnt plastic.

We were lucky. Only a one-foot section of my sleeping pad was singed. I had imagined a burning pyre of tent nylon, our expedition up in flames. No tent, no expedition. All because of our inattention to one crucial detail.

In reality, the fire was over almost before it started. The only aftereffect was the adrenaline surging through our veins. It was apparent that a pump component had contracted in the cold and caused the leak. We'd have to keep the pumps warm. From that point on, each of us slept with a pump every night. During the day we marched with pumps in our pockets. We kept three pumps in reserve.

That night the temperature dropped to -45° F. Our bottle of Scotch froze solid.

The next morning Christina walked over to our tent. She'd been traveling the same route and was camped nearby.

"I'm going back to Ward Hunt," she said. "Both of my stove pumps broke. I'm done."

We assessed her situation—broken stove pumps, her sled too heavy, and her food too high in sugar. It wasn't easy to find the best words. I've rarely been in a position to comfort someone who might be abandoning her life's dream. I gave her an honest hug and turned north.

By the time John and I walked back to retrieve our second pulks, Christina was gone. Her discarded food lay piled on the snow.

"Do you think we'd still be unsupported if we took some cocoa?" I wondered out loud.

"Nah," John said. "We shouldn't risk it."

"Damn." We clipped the carabiners to our pulks and left the pile untouched.

Ice jaw. John walks back to his sled.

Slow train. Day 4, 2:30 p.m.

We walked through the ice clutter, wandering from landmark to landmark, and found ourselves in a junkyard of car-sized boulders frozen at every conceivable angle. On the undersides of a few boulders hung strange icicles covered in gigantic, delicate frost crystals.

During the second march of the day—we divided our travel day into marches lasting an hour and a half to two hours—I snapped one of my snowshoe binding straps. I added a strap extender and that did the trick. Again my boot gaiters were to blame—they were too big for the existing strap.

Later in the day we walked into our first dead end. John was leading. He rounded a corner, disappearing behind an ice boulder that resembled an upright dump truck. I skirted the megalith and found him staring at a jumbled occlusion of boulders eight feet tall. We'd have to go up and over. This was the first of many times that it took both of us working together to move our pulks forward.

In that first week we were working well together but there was some residual tension between us. Unaccountably, some of it slipped out of me in little comments that I regretted even at the time. Most of the tension went away when we began cooperating: hauling, heaving, and negotiating the mayhem of ice formations.

At times we pulled both sleds, but most often we'd haul one forward, drop it and go back to retrieve the other, making every mile into three. The walk back provided some of the most pleasant moments of the day. John and I would catch up with each other's thoughts while gazing at the mountains of Ellesmere silhouetted against the twilight.

We knew that the appearance of the sun would likely warm the upper atmosphere and push the coldest air down to us on the ice. On the morning of Day 5 it happened—our thermometer bottomed out at -60° F. Around noon we saw the full orb of the sun for the first time. What a sight to behold, the sunrise of an entire season.

"Here it is, baby!" John shouted. "The coldest sun on Earth." We sat on our sleds gazing south, trying in vain to absorb the rays.

For the next forty-eight hours the temperature never rose above -50° F. When breaking camp one of those mornings, our feet got dangerously cold. We ran laps around the tent trying to force blood into our toes. Laughing, we wondered what an onlooker would think of the scene. The running only helped a little bit. Hauling could not come soon enough. It took the whole first march to

Dump truck chunk.

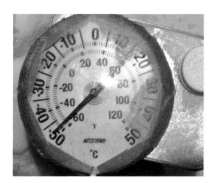

-56° F. The morning of Day 5. Not our coldest reading, but close.

Cold break.

Coldest sun on earth. The first sun rays of the season, -50° F.

Going up.

fully warm our feet.

That first week was all about survival. A case of frostbite could send us home.

During the day we stayed fairly warm while moving. For the most part we were comfortable with two or three layers of Brynje long underwear and our breathable Bergans wind layer. When we stopped for a break, the cold crept in. Fortunately, our appetites had yet to hit overdrive and we were happy to get moving after a quick snack.

As we sat in the tent cooking or eating, only one half of our bodies would get warm. The side facing the stove would warm up and dry out, while the side exposed to the tent wall would grow damp and cold. The ceiling of the tent was dry and hot. The wet upper walls transitioned to a shell of ice that built up around the lower walls. At -50° F we burned our stoves for ten minutes after dinner to give us some extra warmth.

We took extra care to patiently follow our routines and avoid mistakes. Our fuel pumps hadn't leaked since the fire of Day 2, but there were a few other annoyances. I'd been fighting a good cough ever since Iqaluit. The skin of John's fingertips had begun to crack, a common occurrence for him on polar trips. Sadly, one morning I had accidentally left behind a roll of toilet paper that would never fulfill its intended purpose.

But these were minor issues. We now knew firsthand why many expeditions fail in the first week. So far on our scorecard we had an impaired ski binding, a broken snowshoe strap, a nearly disastrous stove fire, and two fleece jackets frozen

Icicle sunrise.

stiff with sweat. Nevertheless, we felt we could take these hurdles in stride.

Day 6 was ridiculously slow, but fun. Rubble was entertaining, with decisions to make at every turn. John and I were completely dialed in. We felt like two youngsters in a giant playground maze. During one break we climbed onto a massive ridge twenty feet high. I aimed my video camera toward John: "Ice armageddon," he said. "Can you imagine the forces that created this mess?" I panned out to the fields of rubble extending in all directions. Seven hours of travel that day netted us 0.97 nm.

We camped at 83° 15' N, 74° 03' W. Nine nautical miles down, four hundred and seven to go. We reminded each other to be patient. We were on schedule. Sjur Mørdre, one of our advisors, had told us to approach the first two weeks as training: survive, be safe, become efficient, and then increase the pace. That was our mentality, but we longed for open spaces and bigger days.

TYLER'S JOURNAL / DAY 6

Again cold. No sweating today. The rubble was monstrous. As if some giant piled up boulders just to prevent our passage. Up and down. Footing was treacherous. As if a mountain had collapsed in front of us.

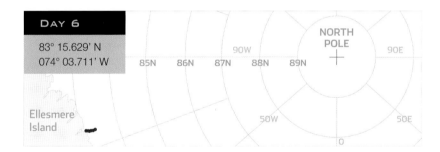

Ice armageddon.

BY JOHN HUSTON

The principles that go into making clothing for polar travel haven't changed in hundreds of years. We had a closet full of synthetic fabrics to choose from, but in some cases the traditional materials were still our preferred choice. The most basic function of clothing for polar ski expeditions is to keep a person as warm and dry as possible. Pulling a three-hundred-pound load generates a lot of body heat, so during the travel day we were happy with a few layers of long underwear and a thin, breathable shell layer on the outside. Our only Michelin Man–like items were insulated boot gaiters, sleeping bags, and down vests to wear on really cold breaks and around camp.

In selecting our clothes we typically look for the following qualities, all of which help keep us warm, dry and happy:

Insulated campwear, Day 2. Tyler uses his big mittens to fill the snow bag. The down vest insulates his core. Knee pads built into his pants insulate his knees from the snow.

INSULATION We wore one or two layers of thin, polypropylene mesh long underwear beneath a thin double layer of polypropylene and wool. Our Brynje mesh long underwear looked atypical, but its capacity to trap air and wick away moisture is the best we've found.

BREATHABILITY Our Bergans of Norway jackets and pants were made of a breathable, non-waterproof lightweight microfiber. In our experience, waterproof breathable fabrics like Gore-Tex stop breathing at temperatures near 0° F. Any fabric that doesn't breathe enough leads to a buildup of frost or ice, leaving a person damp and cold. We didn't need our shell layer to be waterproof because temperatures would always be well below freezing.

WEIGHT It's easy to forget about the weight of your clothing, but just like any other piece of gear it adds up. Lightweight layers gave us the versatility and freedom of movement that heavier clothing could not. Over the course of the expedition it felt like our clothes gained weight as grime built up in the fibers.

For a full clothing list see Appendix 2 on page 164.

Bottom layer, Day 24. John removes a layer of long underwear to keep from overheating on the march.

Baggy Bergans. Airflow, adjustability on the go, and ease of movement are key. John, Day 41.

CIRCULATION Loose-fitting clothing enables both air circulation and blood circulation. Air circulation reduces sweating. Our outer clothing had armpit zippers and leg zippers that allowed us to modulate airflow around the body. Maintaining blood circulation is the key to keeping the extremities warm. Clothing that is too tight can lead to frigid hands or feet.

COMFORT If you're going to wear one set of long underwear for thirty-five days straight, it had better be comfortable. A poor fit can result in constriction or chafing, both of which could've been major annoyances given the length of the trip and the repetitive motions required.

VERSATILITY Our clothing needed to keep us warm and dry in all sorts of weather conditions: at -60° F, at -30° F and windy, and at -10° F and calm and sunny. Adding or subtracting a thin layer of long underwear, and once in a while a layer of fleece, was all we needed to adjust to these different conditions.

DURABILITY Snow at cold temperatures is very abrasive and can trash even tough fabrics. The less time we spent sewing the better. Mostly it was just patching a small hole in a mitten, but a big tear can take a long time to sew. We did a lot of kneeling, working with the sleds and setting up the tent, so a durable pair of pants was essential.

Comfort zone. Tyler's ruff wards off the wind and creates a little area of warmth near his face.

Tyler adjusts his foot layers. Getting this right is well worth it.

Durable duds. Our Bergans outerwear took all the punishment we gave it. John crawls over a ridge, Day 29.

On a trip like this, clothing pretty much becomes part of your body. The only time we noticed it was when something was wrong. Well-placed pockets, an intelligently designed hood, practically positioned flies, and zippers that didn't get stuck went a long way to make our days enjoyable.

By Dr. Helen Findlay

Lord Kingsland Fellow, Plymouth Marine Laboratory, Plymouth, England

Sea ice is simply frozen ocean water. It forms, grows, and melts in the ocean. Perennial sea ice, or multiyear ice, is believed to have existed in the Arctic for at least the last 700,000 years (Worsely & Herman 1980) and could possibly have been present for the last four million years (Clark 1982). Arctic sea ice reaches maximum coverage in early March and recedes back to its minimum extent in September. New ice, or "first-year ice," is ice that forms each year and tends to be between a few centimeters and two meters thick, while multiyear ice can build up to more than four meters in thickness.

Scientists are interested in sea ice because of its importance for regulating climate (Serreze & Barry 2005). Sea ice has a bright surface, which reflects back into space much of the sunlight that hits it. If a greater amount of sea ice melts with warming temperatures, over time there will be fewer bright surfaces available to reflect the solar energy back into space. More energy will be absorbed by the dark oceans, which have a low level of reflectance, causing temperatures to rise further and starting a cycle of increasing warming and melting.

Sea ice also contributes to the ocean's global circulation system (Maykut 1986). When sea ice forms, most of the salt in the water is pushed out of the ice into the ocean below. Water below the sea ice has a higher concentration of salt and is denser than the surrounding seawater and sinks. As cold, dense polar water sinks and moves along the bottom of the oceans toward the equator, warm water from mid-depths to the surface travels from the equator to the poles (and is the reason Europe is relatively warm). Changes in the amount of sea ice forming and melting can disrupt these normal circulation patterns, which in turn impacts the climate we experience in Northern Europe and North America.

Since 1979 satellites have closely monitored the extent of seasonal sea ice. Before this time the best records for sea ice extent came from whaling ships and polar expeditions dating to before the 1800s. Scientists have been able to observe how the sea ice has been changing in the Arctic Ocean (Fetterer et al. 2009). Most notably, the overall area covered by sea ice each year has decreased. Between 1979 and 2009 the summer sea ice cover decreased by more than nine percent per decade. Trends for March are smaller but still show a decrease in extent by nearly three percent per decade. The general scientific opinion is that the Arctic Ocean will be "ice-free" in the summer within the next thirty to fifty years, primarily as a result of greenhouse warming. Sea ice will always form in the winter but high temperatures in the spring and summer

Dr. Helen Findlay.

Courtesy of Dr. Helen Findlay

September 21, 2005

Minimum sea-ice extent.

Orange line indicates median minimum ice edge, 1979–2000.

The black cross indicates the geographic North Pole.

For notes, see Appendix 4, page 167.

September 16, 2007

Minimum sea-ice extent.

February 28, 2009

Sea-ice extent, the maximum extent for 2009.

September 1, 2009

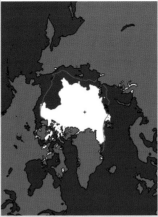

Minimum sea-ice extent.

September 19, 2010

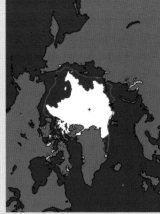

Minimum sea-ice extent.

September 9, 2011

Minimum sea-ice extent.

All sea ice images courtesy of the National Snow and Ice Data Center, University of Colorado, Boulder

will mean little or no ice will survive the melt period. As more ice melts, there will be less ice surviving for multiple years, resulting in an overall loss of thick multiyear ice and a switch to a first-year ice system (Rothrock et al. 1999).

Sea ice has been pivotal in polar exploration (Mulvaney 2001). It was one of the main reasons expeditions failed in their attempts to discover the Northwest Passage between the early 1500s and 1906, when it was finally successfully navigated by Roald Amundsen. Early shipgoing expeditions to the North Pole failed because of sea ice, and it was only by traversing on top of the ice that the North Pole was finally reached. Modern expeditions take place during the maximum sea ice extent in March and April, when they are least likely to encounter open leads, open water, or melt ponds.

The changes taking place in the Arctic Ocean are causing expeditions to more frequently encounter open leads and thinner new ice, while changes in climatic conditions have more recently caused expeditions to be cancelled because of storms, drifting snow, and unsuitable ice for landing planes. This will only worsen in the future, until eventually the

window of opportunity for traversing the sea ice will be too narrow. New adventures will lie in getting across the ice-free Arctic Ocean in summer.

Small changes in climate can, more importantly, have dramatic consequences for the people who live in those environments and depend on natural resources. Many communities in the Arctic rely on the sea ice for hunting and transportation. If the sea ice melts too quickly in spring, it shortens the hunting season and means that northern communities rely more and more on modern food, technology, and economics. Communities must rapidly adapt to new ways of living, but are doing so at the loss of traditions and culture. With the Arctic potentially ice-free in summer, industry and commercial organizations are already turning their heads North. The oil and gas industries are seeking to exploit new reserves, fishing industries new fish stocks, and shipping industries shorter shipping routes. These additional exploitations of resources will add stress to an already fragile system. The benefits from these new resources will come at an environmental cost, as the Arctic will remain a challenging and hostile environment, increasing the risk of manmade disasters during the winter ice and periods of severe weather.

"The inevitable always happens." —Tyler Fish

On Day 7, the temperature rose to -38° F. It felt like spring.

Thanks to the warming, our pulks slid a lot easier. Each of us could now pull two pulks at once for almost the entire day. For some reason the ice was more relaxed—that is, under less pressure—and not nearly as jumbled. The day before, we'd struggled mightily to cover only 0.97 nm. By the end of Day 7 we had somehow covered 3.9 nm in only six hours and fifty minutes, besting our previous record by 1.3 nm.

That evening in the tent, between slurps of glistening pemmican stew, we rehashed our progress. "Wow," John said, "what a mess that was yesterday. I'm thinking that must've been from two big floes colliding."

"Hmm, could be."

"If that's the case, maybe the terrain will be more open from now on."

"We can only hope."

Hope on the ice is a fragile thing. If our hopes rose one day due to easier terrain, they were often dashed the next. After Day 7 the amount of rubble diminished, but we ran into a new set of obstacles: snow features formed by the wind.

Sastrugi—grooves or ridges formed as snowpack is built up and eroded irregularly by the wind—became our energy-zapping nemesis. They ranged from two to six feet high and came in a wide variety of shapes laid out in unending fields perpendicular to our path of travel. The smaller undercut ridges were annoying but relatively easy to snowshoe across. We called the larger sastrugi snow dunes. These were a problem. Uninterrupted travel through fields of head-high snow dunes taxed our energy more than anything we'd faced thus far.

On Day 7, we devised a new shuttling strategy, one we had used to portage canoes and packs in Minnesota. The leader pulled one large pulk forward for ten minutes. Leaving the other large pulk behind, the follower hitched the two small pulks together, hauled them forward for five minutes and parked them. While the leader continued ahead, the follower walked back to the other large pulk and brought it all the way forward. Meanwhile, the first person returned to the two small pulks and brought them all the way forward. This way we traveled only two steps for each step forward.

Our legs ached with the effort. We couldn't go too fast, or we'd end up with sore muscles from a buildup of lactic acid. Nor did we want to sweat. Damp clothes would only chill us later. Our pace was constant and tortoise-like.

Clockwise from top left: **Moonrise.** Looking east, Day 9, 5:37 p.m. • **John.** Day 9, 5:37 p.m. • **Sunset.** Looking southwest, Day 9, 5:37 p.m.   71

Sastrugi. Tyler heads into a set of our beloved snow waves.

Fading coast. Tyler packs up camp on the morning of Day 11. The mountains of Ellesmere Island are barely visible from a ridge twenty feet above the ice.

During the afternoon of Day 8, John switched to skis for the first time since Day 1.

"Fish," he shouted from out front. "This is just awesome."

As I snowshoed closer he continued, "Dude, maybe we should stop and fix your ski binding."

"Let's wait. I'd rather deal with it in the tent." I didn't think it was a good idea at -34° F.

"Yeah, you're right."

I was used to tempering John's enthusiasm, which tended to bubble over. That was the way he operated, throwing out ideas all the time. My approach to problem solving was more contemplative. Working together, we struck a good balance most of the time.

For the rest of the day he skied and I snowshoed. His pace was only slightly faster than mine, but I knew he was expending less energy.

That night I fixed my binding. I used my Victorinox SwissTool to pare away the part of the gaiter that sat too far forward on the boot. I also added a heel cable to the binding to ensure that my toe didn't slip out.

We began Day 9 on skis. We hauled both pulks most of the day but netted only 3.4 nm in eight hours.

Day 10 was warmer, -22° F, but the breeze from the east-northeast bit into our exposed skin. We surprised ourselves by breaking the 4.0-nm barrier, covering 4.7 nm in eight hours and twenty minutes.

TYLER'S JOURNAL / DAY 11

I felt a little down yesterday. Sleds were heavy for me. I felt leading wasn't for me, so instead I zoned out behind. Maybe this was from the poor visibility.

We were making progress. Ward Hunt Island was out of sight. Now there were no familiar landmarks, and nothing inscribed on a map could match what we were experiencing.

A strange mix of strength, balance, and speed is required to haul two pulks across a field of snow dunes. Approaching a rise, you lean forward with all the

Sastrugi sequence. Lean. Grunt. Step. Lean. Pop it over. Get out of the way.

Snow ramp. John skis over a ridge.

weight of your body and backpack. Leaning at a ridiculous angle over your ski tips, you push with both poles till you finally top the crest. Then you feel the first pulk rise over the lip and begin its downward slide, easing the second pulk up and over. You sprint a few strides to get out of the way of the careening pulks. Now repeat this process over and over again, sometimes for a mile at a stretch.

We knew that at some point we would drop our small sleds. Doing this too early would make hauling more difficult. It was a matter of distributing weight

Inner ocean. Day 11, 10:15 a.m.

over the surface area of the two sleds to minimize friction. Too much weight in a single sled would ruin this equation. Once we made the decision there was no going back.

John and I decided to perform a test. On Day 14 we transferred the entire contents of the small sleds to the large ones and towed the empty small ones behind. Right away the sleds bogged down. Halfway into the first march we stopped and reloaded.

A few hours later, the Arctic Ocean funneled us straight into a massif, a gargantuan rubble formation that John immediately named The Colossus.

It was early afternoon—windy, hazy, overcast, and -30° F. John was a bit ahead of me. I'd nearly caught up with him when he motioned for me to go over a ridge to my left. I assumed this was a shortcut. The ridge was at least twenty feet high, but it looked doable.

I lashed my skis to the top of the large pulk and left it at the base of the ridge. Then I climbed up, pulling the small pulk up behind me. I negotiated the numerous stages to the top, heaved the pulk over the rim and down the other side, and nestled it onto some refrigerator-sized blocks of ice.

"That was brutal," I thought to myself. "Where is John? Why did he send me here?" Sometimes it was hard to be the second skier for this reason. You just had to trust the person in front.

I went back for my large pulk. Halfway up the ridge, I realized it was stupid to try to maneuver it by myself. Eventually, John appeared and made his way over to help me.

We stood together next to my pulks and looked around. It was as if we were in a Western movie and we'd ridden our horses into a blind canyon. A quick assessment of the surrounding walls told us we should leave the pulks and survey the scene from higher up.

"Higher up" felt like a different movie, as if we were overlooking the ruins of some bombed-out European town during World War II. We gazed in every direction but couldn't see any way around or through.

At least this hulking mess wasn't moving. We agreed that straight through was our best course—first with the small pulks, then with the large ones.

We figured it out as we went. It was like we were mountaineering, but without crampons, ice axes, or ropes. We lifted, heaved, and helped each other with the sleds. To the north, the weather looked dark gray and ominous. The breeze had been a biting one. But in here it was calm and quiet, and we forgot about everything else.

Looking west. The Colossus.

Looking east. The Colossus.

Passageway. Tyler.

Halfway through. Tyler.

Toward the end. The easy part.

We were in The Colossus for four hours, patiently picking our way toward the other side.

That morning the ocean had been a broad expanse of gentle snow dunes. It now consisted of tight bluish passageways through ice blocks precariously stacked several stories high. Normally we traveled on top of the Arctic Ocean. Now we were inside of it. Boulders could break loose and crush us. One slip might break a leg or knock one of us unconscious.

Despite the danger, this was the best type of work. We entered a zone of total focus. Time disappeared.

Sometimes we would lean forward at an extreme angle, straining on the sled traces with all of our strength and body weight. Other times we needed all four hands on one sled to advance it without putting ourselves in peril.

Eventually we made it out. Our six-unit team of people and pulks had gone through the wringer and come out better for it. Our communication had been perfect. It seemed like much of the old mental baggage was now buried amid the blue ice of The Colossus.

To the north the weather looked sinister. Blustery winds swept across an expanse of nearly snowless ice that led to a heavy, dark horizon.

Meditative mood. Tyler.

That evening it took us a while to find enough hard-packed snow to stake the tent. Once inside we revisited the day's events, satisfied with covering only 3.2 nm.

It was Sunday, the day we designated for our once-a-week satellite phone calls home. We called it Family Day. I would phone Sarah, and John would phone Jennifer. Although we limited the conversations to thirty minutes or less, the good thoughts lingered for days.

Days 15 and 16 finally saw our pace increase, likely due to the flattening terrain. We made personal bests of 4.8, then 6.0 nm, traveling eight and a half hours each day.

First day I didn't take my skis off for the whole day! This is a significant change.

We'd settled into the peculiar meditative rhythm of skiing slowly and thinking slowly for hours on end. In this mode we were never sure what was on the other person's mind. If I was singing, John had a pretty good idea of my mood. He was harder for me to read from a distance, although up close I could always tell by the

Masked up. Tyler at the end of Day 16.

Evening, Day 17. Site of the first celebratory Scotch toast.

intensity of his gaze whether he was thinking or just *being* out there.

In two hours of skiing, any number of topics would cross and re-cross my mind. How's our pace? Is that open water ahead? God, I hope not. When do we bump up the calories, please? What's our fuel ration now? (A math problem ensues.) Where's John? I think my mask is frozen to my face. When do we cross the next degree of latitude? I wonder what Sarah and Ethan are doing. When you're in a blissful state of non-thinking, or distracted by memories and daydreams, a ninety-minute march can go by in a flash.

On a long expedition there's a significant amount of time spent just patiently working your way toward the inevitable. There will be another side to this dune field. The weather will turn—for the better or worse. The day will end. I will take my backpack off. I will sit down. Soupy dinner in my mug will warm my hands. Sleep will come.

At the end of Day 17 we basked in the warmth of our tent, having covered 6.9

nm and crossed 84° N. That night John poured a half-shot of Scotch into each of our one-liter dinner mugs and we toasted the accomplishment. It was the first of our degree-crossing celebrations.

The next morning we set our sights on 85° N. There were six more degrees of latitude to the Pole. In the next thirty-eight days we'd need to travel 360 nautical miles. It had taken us seventeen days to cover the first fifty-six.

Turning to the goal of increasing our daily progress, we upped our travel time to nine and a half hours per day. We were careful, though, not to push too hard too soon.

On Day 16 we had followed the preset schedule and bumped our rations from 5,700 calories to 6,700 calories per day. Mealtime was sacred. I explained this in one of the nightly blog entries we dictated via satellite phone: "You can imagine us every morning and every evening holding our hot, soupy breakfast or dinner, cradling it for warmth. We turn off the stove to save fuel. So we both sit here in the cold, holding it and eating it, and both of those feel good." But oh, how we wished for a second helping.

This desire for more was an intense feeling, a true hunger, and an indicator that our metabolisms were nearing full throttle. It was as if an insatiable animal lived in each of our stomachs, an animal that would do anything to get more calories. If it didn't take in enough food, this clever beast would steal from our fat reserves, and then our muscles. We knew this would happen eventually, but we wanted to preserve muscle mass for as long as possible.

We had a mix of weather in that third week. Clear skies gave way to clouds and warmer temperatures (-28° to -20° F), but side winds stabbed at our faces.

First thing in the morning John would leave the tent to perform what he referred to as a "poosh," his term for swiftly heeding the call of nature in tough conditions.

I could hear him in the distance: "Cold!"

I'd yell to him, "What kind of day is it? Mask day?"

"Mask day. Big time."

These neoprene masks provided low-maintenance armor for our faces. Outside the tent we'd often wear them all day. We had modified the masks with enlarged mouth holes, but for me, drinking and eating were still a bit of a challenge.

We'd budgeted fifteen minutes for every rest stop, but neither one of us wanted to spend much time huddled in the faint lee of some lonely ice chunk. Conversations were brief. Our efforts to get at the food and water in our pulks would be punctuated with grunts, loud sighs, and the occasional whoop. Get out of the wind. Get food in. Get pee out. Take a picture? No. Cold hands. Can we leave now? When it was time to go, John liked to say, "Shake and bake!"

The theme, I guess, is optimistic patience. This expedition is front-loaded with a lot of heavy work. We just have to be patient and know that our loads will decrease and the friction on our sleds will decrease, too, and that we'll be able to travel more miles later. We're confident in that. We just have to keep reminding ourselves that each day is a new opportunity to get closer to the North Pole.

On breaks the cold would seep in. I'd feel the pain most keenly in my hands. If I didn't do anything about it they would get weak and clumsy—or worse, numb—unable to operate a zipper.

To force the warm blood into his hands, John would flap his arms about his

Morning steps. Tyler's view through the tent door, 5:09 a.m.

Hydration station.

Dog sleds. Tyler named his sleds after his dogs so that he wouldn't get mad at them.

Snotsicle. Our noses ran constantly. Nothing to do but let it flow. John, Day 14.

Training payoff. Same motion, but now on the ocean.

torso and grunt. I'm not sure what the grunting accomplished, but the movement was essential. I'd swing one arm around overhead like a swimmer doing the backstroke and swing the opposite arm forward. With a little warmth creeping back into our hands, we'd start skiing again. It could take half an hour or more to warm them back up.

Once in a while on calm, relatively "warm" days, we could relax a bit. During one break on a -30° F day, John sat on the back of his pulk, resting out of the wind, facing the sun. "You don't know how cold it was until the cold is gone. It was cold back then," he said with a chuckle as he chewed on bacon and butter, snot streaming out of his nose. Our noses were almost always running. It's a fact of polar travel.

On the morning of Day 20 we came across a recently frozen lead embedded with fresh polar bear tracks—a mother and two cubs. The tracks were heading south, which told us the bears might have passed within a mile of our tent the night before. The mother's prints measured over twelve inches long. At least they were heading the opposite direction. Bear encounters on this part of the Arctic Ocean

were rare, but given that a polar bear can pick up a scent from thirty miles away, we were cautious. For the next several days we skied closer together, but saw no sign of bears.

Our daily distances were respectable, but we wanted to cover more territory. On Day 21 we registered 5.4 nm in nine and a half hours.

"Slow and steady," one of us would say.

"Slow and steady," the other would repeat. It was our mantra.

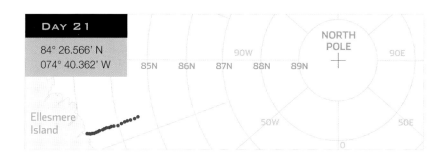

DAY 21

84° 26.566' N
074° 40.362' W

NORTH POLE

85N 86N 87N 88N 89N 90W 90E

Ellesmere Island

50W 50E

By Tyler Fish

A century ago and earlier, explorers would leave home and not be heard from 'til they turned up to declare they'd discovered new places. Nowadays, explorers post up-to-the-minute expedition data on the Internet. However, this convenience comes at a price. Our yearning to embrace a simple, uncluttered lifestyle is one reason we go on expeditions. Trying to keep the outside world informed can get in the way. On this trip we felt torn between the freedom of the expedition and our responsibility to the folks back home. But we always knew that communication and documentation were a must, for safety reasons and to keep our audience informed.

Our Devices

Iridium satellite phones
(Two, 368 g each)
They never let us down. All of our communication with the outside world went through these phones. One was a backup.

HP iPaq PDA
(202 g)
Winner of the "Total Pain in the Ass Award," this device was temperamental at best. At various times it wouldn't charge, connect, send, receive, or sync. We don't like thinking about the hours of sleep and relaxation we lost just trying to upload pictures to our blogs.

Solara tracking device
(650 g)
Forty-eight hours of no communication would automatically activate our rescue protocols, so we bought this little black brick as a backup in case our satellite phones went down. It was designed to transmit our position and send text messages. We tested it, but fortunately we didn't have to use it.

Canon G10 digital cameras
(Two, 400 g each)
We loved our G10s. We each carried one in a chest pocket for easy access. These cameras were the true storytellers of the expedition, recording pictures, video, and audio.

Sony HDR-CX12 video camera
(544 g)
We really wanted to take more video, but the cold kept zapping the battery. Though it was one of the smallest high-definition cameras on the market, it was a little too big to carry conveniently in a warm pocket.

ACR personal locator beacon
(322 g)
In case of a life and death emergency, we could've turned this beacon on to transmit our location via satellite and notify the authorities.

> *"Oh, for the good ol' days."*
>
> —John Huston, again wishing he had been born in the past.

For the full equipment list see Appendix 2, page 164.

Tech daddy. Tyler's father at work with our video camera and chargers.

Dispatch, Day 10. Tyler calls in the blog and route information using our Iridium satellite phone.

Tyler with John's nemesis. Tapping out an email on the iPaq.

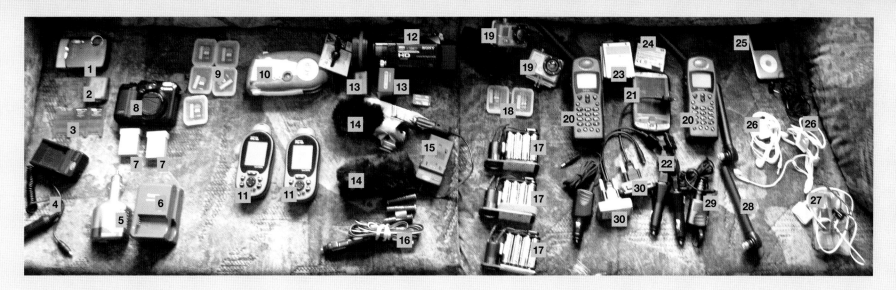

1. Olympus u790SW Camera

2. Extra Battery for Olympus Camera

3. Olympus Memory Cards with Card Holder

4. 12V DC Charger for Olympus Camera Batteries

5. DC/AC Converter

6. 120V AC Charger for Canon G10 Batteries

7. Extra Batteries for Canon G10 Camera

8. Canon G10 Camera

9. Canon G10 Camera Memory Cards

10. ACR Emergency Beacon

11. DeLorme PN-40 GPS

12. Sony HDR-CX12 Video Camera

13. Extra Batteries for Sony HDR-CX12 Video Camera

14. Video Camera Microphones with Wind Cover

15. 12V DC Charger for Sony HDR-CX12 Batteries

16. Cables for Video Camera Battery Charger

17. 8AA Custom Battery Charger with Batteries

18. GoPro Hero Memory Cards

19. GoPro Hero Video Camera

20. Iridium Satellite Phone 9505A

21. HP iPaq

22. 12V DC Charger for HP iPaq

23. Extra Batteries for Iridium Satellite Phone 9505A

24. Battery for HP iPaq

25. Apple iPod

26. Headphones

27. Apple iPod Wired Remote

28. Extra Antennas for Iridium Satellite Phone 9505A

29. 12V DC Chargers for Iridium Satellite Phone 9505A

30. Data Cables for Iridium Satellite Phone 9505A

BY TYLER FISH

Taking care of yourself is a skill, something that takes commitment and self-discipline. Every expedition environment pushes you to learn it again and again. You must ask yourself: How do I take care of myself now?

To be safe on a polar expedition, you must establish healthy routines and adapt proactively to the cold.

John and I each had our own routines. If we were managing the simple steps to take care of our bodies, we were comfortable.

"It's a self-care expedition."

—John Huston

CHECKLIST FOR A GOOD DAY

• Try to empty your bowels first thing in the morning. For those who want to know—and the question always comes up—we just kicked a little hole in the snow and made as if we were using a squat toilet. Normally the butt doesn't get cold, but the hands sometimes do.

• Floss and brush your teeth once a day—twice and you're doing really well. Suck on the toothbrush before brushing so you don't break off the frozen bristles.

• When traveling, pee wherever and whenever you want.

• Apply Dermatone Z-Cote (zinc oxide) sunscreen to your face. Rub Dermatone lip balm on your nose and lips.

• Tape your feet with zinc athletic tape to prevent blisters.

• Take your vitamins.

• Wipe your nose on a cotton bandana after coming into the tent at night.

• Stretch every third day.

• Take a sponge bath every third day. Kit: small synthetic cloth in a plastic bag.

• Dry out your mittens, hats, and masks every night. Finish in the morning.

• Pee in a bottle when in the tent. Empty it through a hole in the tent floor. At night pee in a bottle inside your sleeping bag and make sure you dump out the bottle, or close it and sleep with it. Otherwise you'll end up with a big mess or a frozen bottle of pee.

Mask and ruff. John. Day 11.

Happy feet. We took meticulous care of our feet. Each night we let them dry out, then washed them with a small rag.

Tape-up. Dry, cracked fingers plagued John for much of the trip.

Tyler's toothbrush.

WHAT DOES COLD FEEL LIKE?

The sensation of cold can hit you on a rainy day at 40° F or on the ice at -40° F. On a polar expedition, it is usually focused on a body part—typically the hands, feet, or face. You have to be willing to change what you're doing in order to warm up. It takes perspective and self-discipline to be proactive about it.

When you start to feel cold, first there's a twinge of pain in the toes or fingers that usually feel it the most. Then it spreads like a slow dip into water, but with the pain of fire.

Skilled polar explorers know how to push the edges of cold tolerance without serious injury. Only from experience do you gain the mindset that enables you to adapt and stay safe. Most often, adapting means adding a layer or removing a layer, eating, drinking, or stimulating circulation through vigorous movement.

When I started to get too cold on this expedition, I'd often say to myself, "I'm okay, I'm okay, I'm okay." I was constantly checking to see how much longer I could continue what I was doing (taking a photo, playing with the GPS, packing up the tent, etc.) without stopping and actively warming up. My feet got cold in the morning, my fingers during breaks, and my face when it got windy or when I was skiing near open water. Cold is an unseen beast that can find the chink in any armor. It's up to us to plug the holes, put up our shield, or push it back.

Number 1. Tyler's pee bottle in use. We poured urine right into the snow through a small hole in the tent floor.

Number 2. A little shelter is better than no shelter.

7 THE SIMPLE LIFE

BY TYLER FISH

"The weeks passed. We saw no sign of either a ship or of drifting remains to show that there were other people in the world. The whole sea was ours, and with all the gates of the horizon open, real peace and freedom wafted down from the firmament itself.

"It was as though the fresh salt tang in the air, and all the blue purity that surrounded us, had washed and cleansed both body and soul. To us on the raft the great problems of civilized man appeared false and illusory, mere perverted products of the human mind." —Thor Heyerdahl, *Kon-Tiki*

This trip would be the longest trip of my life. John was concerned that the length of it would demoralize me at some point, but I knew this wouldn't happen.

I love the constant physical and mental engagement of expeditioning. The easy focus and sense of purpose are addictive. There's an exhilarating blend of the unknown and the predictable. Relationships with others are full of substance. No one can fake it. Conversations go deeper. There are tangible consequences to everything we do.

The longer I'm out there, the better it gets. For me there is no better way to live completely in the present. I love the simple rhythms of the journey. It's like losing yourself while singing a song or a playing a sport. I usually drag my feet coming home, in no rush to complicate my life again.

The rhythm of this expedition was created by our deliberate routines.

John would lead the first two marches of the day. He always wanted to get moving and warm up his feet. I might snap a few photos before following him out of camp. Generally, I had the best energy in the morning, John in the afternoon. Both of us were game for the whole day, but we were "on" at different times.

John always picked the campsite for the night. The ideal spot was a relatively

Sundown camp. Our favorite time of day.

Humble abode.

flat piece of hard-packed snow where the stakes could sink in and hold.

It took ten to twenty minutes to set up the tent. Once we staked it out, John crawled inside, raised the center pole, and swept snow off the floor with a handheld brush. Outside, I shoveled snow onto the snow flaps. When covered with an eight-inch layer of granular snow, these flaps kept the wind out and the tent walls taut and secure.

Downtime. Tyler takes a mid-afternoon break.

While John arranged gear inside, I hunted for densely packed snow, the most efficient for melting into water. The denser the snow, the less fuel we'd use. I stomped around, probing with the shovel, and loaded a nylon stuff sack with pieces that would fit neatly into our "Fat Lady" teapot.

I liked to linger a bit while searching for just the right snow, my last outdoor task of the day. It was my time with the quiet of the ocean. Soon I'd be in the tent with boots off and stoves roaring away. Delaying the luxury of the tent just a little longer made it sweeter.

Returning, I dropped the two snow bags next to the doorway. "I'm ready."

"Okay," John said from inside as he loosened the drawstrings. Then I stuck my head in and said, "Hello."

"Hello." It was like he was welcoming me home.

I banged and brushed the snow off my boots, crawled in, pulled in a snow bag, and cinched the door shut.

I'd just gone from the widest open space on the frozen skin of the planet to the tiniest closed-in room you'd ever want to spend a night in. Agoraphobia or claustrophobia—neither would do on this trip.

Next was our favorite ritual, the lighting of the stoves. It went like this:

John set out the stove board.

One of us announced, "Open bottle" (so we'd keep still to prevent spillage). Then we:

Opened the bottles and attached the fuel pumps, one bottle at a time.

Pumped the bottles to pressurize the fuel.

Attached the bottles to the stoves.

Released a few drops of fuel into the stoves' reservoirs.

One of us called, "Fire it up!"

The other responded, "Fire it up!"

Then we:

Lit the reservoirs to heat the fuel lines, which turned the liquid fuel to gas.

Opened the fuel valve to ignite the burners, which emitted an orange flame that soon receded to a tight, blue, low-hissing roar.

Happy times were here.

Following this sequence over one hundred times since the Day 2 mishap, we didn't spill a single drop of fuel.

The heat spread slowly at first, but soon the cone of the tent's ceiling was well above freezing. We were careful to leave a small opening in the door to pull in some fresh air as heat and fumes exited through the vent at the top of the tent. As the stoves went to work we hung up our hats, masks, mittens and socks.

Every night John served up the pemmican stew hot and soupy. We loved it that way, mostly for the hydration, but also because the added volume gave us the illusion of second helpings. He turned off the stoves right after the cooking was finished.

After dinner, as the tent cooled down, we typically had twenty minutes of free time before bed. One night I'd stretch. The next night I would take a little bath, using a hand-size synthetic cloth to wash and a small plastic bag that served as a miniature sink. Other nights I would sew, write in my journal, or just sit and relax.

Going to bed was a process. First we each straightened up our side of the tent to make room for the sleeping bags, which lay within arm's reach outside the door. As we pulled them in we brushed the frost off—anything to minimize moisture. The outer bag, inner bag, and a Therm-a-Rest sleeping pad all fit together as one unit.

We each wore a dry hat and dry mittens to bed. John wore his facemask to protect his nose. Any items that were still damp we slid inside our bags to be dried by the warmth of our bodies.

We loved sleeping in our down cocoons, but getting into them was a nightmare. We had to grope and fumble our way into the four-layer sleeping system. Inside the inner bag we had two vapor barrier liners (VBLs). They kept our perspiration trapped next to our bodies and out of the sleeping bag insulation. The VBLs also contributed some warmth and weren't nearly as damp as we'd expected. Eventually we'd be snuggled in, zippers up and drawcords cinched, our heads resting on a pillow of fleece jackets.

I didn't sleep alone. Inside the sleeping bags and liners I had my night mittens, a stove pump, my iPod, often the video camera, my Canon G10, and my anti-snoring device in case John hit me during the night. (I come from a long line of snorers, so he'd hit me just about every night.) A one-liter bottle of hot water lay tucked in the foot of my bag.

Falling asleep is never a problem for me. I flip a switch and I'm done. John calls me narcoleptic, but I consider it a superpower. On occasion, though, I'd

Fire it up! John and his cherished box of matches. Lighting the stoves, our favorite ritual, was one of many routines designed for safety and efficiency.

Fat Lady at work. We loved our big teapot.

God natt, Tyler.

God natt, John. For some reason we always said "good night" in Norweigan.

Flat world. Tyler exults.

fall asleep in the midst of wriggling and zipping and wake up with a cold arm hanging out.

In the morning we reversed everything. I always cooked breakfast. We took twenty minutes to journal or make small repairs. Then it was out of the tent and back on our skis. Each day we looked forward to dinner and our warm sleeping bags, only to pop right up seven hours later and start the cycle all over again.

We designed our routines and sleep regimen to keep us healthy. In many ways we saw the expedition as an extended self-care exercise. We dealt proactively with sore feet, sun exposure, and dry skin. One of the great polar ironies is that, despite skiing in -30° weather, overheating can be a major problem.

By Day 23 the sun was higher in the sky, and as the terrain allowed for longer periods of uninterrupted skiing, we began to sweat more. "Sweat is the enemy," John liked to say. At Outward Bound I'd tell my students, "Work is warm. Wet is cold." But work can create sweat, which built up in our clothing in the form of frost. Over the course of a day, the frost would reduce the insulating capacity of our clothes, resulting in cold hands and noses.

Sweat could also lead to inner thigh chafing. John had suffered from this on the way to the South Pole and didn't want to experience it again. For as long as I've known him, he's never liked the heat. On the Arctic Ocean it was once again his nemesis. He'd try to adjust his layers without removing them. He'd open his armpit or leg zippers, take off his shell mittens, and open up his jacket.

Midway into the fourth week we found a really sweet groove. We were skiing over expansive fields of snow, and the season was changing.

Spring on the Arctic Ocean is an enormous relief. Day by day, the sun grows warmer, the light more intense—a welcome contrast to the cold dawn of early March.

These were good times, the kind you want expeditions to be made of. We worked hard and slept well and ate everything we could without stealing from future rations. I tried to spare some chocolate, keeping it in reserve for a few weeks down the road.

The lingering sun had a magical effect. We ended many of our travel days enveloped in a radiant alpenglow. At that time of day the temperature felt perfect and the wind felt soft. We could have skied forever. On Day 26 we netted 7.9 nm, our best mileage to date.

Tyler, Day 25.

Snack attack. Sitting right on 85° N.

That evening we set up camp bathed in golden light. John looked over at me and hollered, "Can you believe this is our world?" Moments like this happened now and then, usually when we were warmed up and well fed and the light was nice. I would think, "Who's living better than us?"

On days like this we were able to laugh at the personal quirks that sometimes made things difficult. I thought John tried to control too much, and John thought I was stubborn, and both of these things were true. Yet we were a solid team. We trusted each other.

JOHN'S JOURNAL / DAY 25

We are getting along better and better as we achieve more, push each other personally and tolerate each other more. We are both good-hearted people and have the good of the team in mind. . . . We come at the world so differently and are both too stubborn to let go easily. But we do.

We crossed 85° N on Day 26. We celebrated with Scotch and a new treat that I concocted of leftover nuts, butter, and a little sugar. Warm it up and spoon it in. It was so nice to taste something sugary and different. We traveled 8.0 nm on Day 28, for a solid week's total of 53.4 nm.

TYLER'S BLOG ENTRY / DAY 27

Right now our expedition is sustainable. We feel really good about the work we've put in. We eat well, we sleep well. We're also calm. We feel like we've been doing the right things and our routines are good. We trust each other and we are going to make it.

When we climbed out of our tents on Day 30 the wind was blowing from the south. Toward the end of the second march I was following John with my head down, lost in thought. When I looked up, a river of open water was blocking our path. John had left his pulks behind and was scouting the lead. There was no obvious way across.

I took out the video camera to document our first open lead. John skied toward me, looking down at his skis as he crossed a small crack in the ice. Without missing a beat he looked up and pointed with his pole. "Oh, look! There's a seal! It just

Soft evening. These conditions made for some truly sweet arrivals into camp.

THE SIMPLE LIFE / 93

ducked under."

A small black dot bobbed in the distance, maybe two hundred feet away. It disappeared for a few seconds and reappeared a little closer. It was poking itself up through the thinnest ice. It was fun to see another living creature out here.

We briefly talked about swimming the lead. A fifty-foot span of open water gave off mist in the middle of it. Dark gray ice that looked wet and weak bordered the open water on both sides. We'd likely have to swim through that ice as well. It seemed like too much to ask for the first swim of the trip. We agreed to ski westward along the edge.

The wind was coming at us from the side. When it was at our backs we hardly felt it, but now it bored into our weak spots. Humidity from the lead seeped through our clothing. As we skied more cautiously our heart rates slowed and less heat reached our extremities. After leading one full march, I was the coldest I'd been in a long time.

We examined the various types of ice. Some, white with frost, was thick and stable. Some, darker and thinner and dotted with frost flowers, flexed under our weight. I wanted to learn more about it. What does weak ice feel like? How does it behave? Where is the line between skiable and getting dunked?

On the next march I stayed in front. I soon found myself skiing along a narrow ledge of good ice, skirting the open water. At my left shoulder was a steep embankment about six feet high, probably the result of a dune that split in half when the lead opened up. The ice ahead was darker, embedded with a scattering of foot-sized chunks of more solid ice.

I moved gingerly onto this jumble, one ski after the other. Within seconds I noticed that one of the ice chunks under my right ski had begun to sink. I transferred all of my weight to my left ski, but I knew it wouldn't hold. Black water swirled over my skis.

Without thinking I fell against the embankment. I clung to the snow with my hands and knees. My feet, still attached to my skis, dangled in the water, but they weren't wet or cold. Not yet. What am I doing? Get up. Keep your skis on. Get out! Somehow I vaulted myself up the wall to safety, six feet above where I'd been hanging on.

Well, now I've tested the ice.

My legs had been submerged to the knees for less than five seconds. My gaiters were getting crunchy as they froze. I used loose snow to sponge up any water visible on my pants and gaiters. My feet were dry. I was fine.

First open lead. No way across, but John gives a thumbs up anyway. Day 30, 9:58 a.m.

The apron. Day 30, 11:41 a.m.

Post soaking. Tyler's crusty bottom half. Thankfully only the outer clothing got wet. Day 30, just after 1:00 p.m.

The crack. Day 30, 2:01 p.m.

John had backtracked and gone behind a huge drift, the intact side of my embankment. Now he reached me, worried. "Well, that was dumb," I said. "Let's not do that again."

"Dude, that could've been really bad!"

"I'm okay. No water got in."

I skied across some rough ice to scrape the slush from the bottoms of my skis and we were on our way.

I was feeling better until I came to a steaming five-foot crack that ran perpendicular to the big lead. At the intersection of the two leads I jumped across, but on takeoff I broke the ice, stranding John on the other side.

He tried using his pulk as a bridge, but when he stood up on it, more ice broke off. He teetered momentarily, almost fell in, and deemed it a bad idea. I assembled a catamaran by connecting the two large pulks with my skis. He crawled across and we continued on.

We skied west for four hours along the big lead until we came to a place where it narrowed, then split open again to the west. At the narrowest point in

Two-pulk bridge. John after crawling across Tyler's improvised catamaran. The lead is to the left, the unjumpable crack to the right. Day 30, 2:01 p.m.

Hard-earned camp. Evening, Day 30.

this bottleneck, a morass of jumbled ice formed a bridge twenty yards long that we thought would support us. We shuttled the pulks across, probing each step with our ski poles. Any part of this slippery conglomeration could be loose and might suddenly shift. Swimming here would be similar to the trash compactor scene in *Star Wars*, complete with moving walls that could crush us.

When we finally reached the northern side, I skied away from the lead with new intensity. I was tired of sparring with it. The Arctic Ocean had just kicked our asses. And we knew it would happen again.

During the last march of the day we spied another big east-west lead, stretching from horizon to horizon. This lead was open too, and we were on the wrong side. We usually liked to camp on the north side of a lead in order to put the obstacle behind us. A lead might grow overnight. Also, open water meant seals, and seals meant bears.

Rather than push it we decided to camp. We were eager to get into the tent, eat dinner, and go to bed. We had only traveled 5.0 nm closer to the Pole.

The next morning, April 1, marked the thirty-first day of the expedition. It was

-36° F and luckily the lead had frozen. We skied across the spongy surface covered with new frost flowers, which felt like skiing on a firm waterbed.

On Day 33 our thermometer read -10° F as it lay in the sun just before we left camp. On a break John took off all his top layers, exposing his bare chest for the first time. "There it is! I'm a skinny boy." John had lost weight. What would he look like a few weeks from now? "Wooooo!" he bellowed.

That day we pushed ahead for an extra thirty minutes and crossed 86° N. The celebration was a high point of the week.

Athletically, John and I were a perfect match. We both had enough speed and endurance to maintain a comfortable cruising pace, and the strength to handle ridges and rubble. This gave us confidence. Without this balance the trip could have turned into a miserable waiting game. Our pace, including breaks, was in line with our goal of one nautical mile per hour.

A few days earlier, Julie Hignell, our safety and logistics manager, had informed us of a huge lead in our path near 87° N. Satellite images showed a swath of humidity oriented southeast to northwest. It was impossible to tell if the lead

Fresh crossing. Tyler makes tracks through some big frost flowers on a frozen lead, Day 31.

Hot John. Sweat is the enemy.

They used to be white. John says goodbye to his liner socks after thirty-two days of use. It was an emotional moment.

Mr. Fix-it. Tyler repairs his delaminating ski tip.

Over the fence. At this point it felt like we were skiing across farm fields separated by fences of rubble.

Goodbye, little pulks. Tyler readies Bud for abandonment.

No one has called yet.

was open or frozen. If it was open, it could stop our progress for days. If it was frozen and oriented north, it could be the ski highway we dreamed of, free of rubble and sastrugi.

On Day 34 we covered 11.2 nm, another best. We were one day ahead of schedule.

The next day we dropped our small sleds. We'd made a test and found that hauling one fully loaded sled apiece slightly improved our pace.

I struggled with the thought of leaving the sleds behind. What a waste. But I'd come to terms with the reality of our situation. Resupplied expeditions, which by definition carry less weight, have a wider margin of success built into them. The extra weight carried by unresupplied expeditions can cut drastically into that margin. As a result, some items have to be abandoned, to eventually end up on the bottom of the ocean. The environmental impact would be small. Still, I was conflicted.

Normally I get a little more sentimental than John, so for me it was harder to say goodbye. Inside the smaller pulk I wrote in big, black letters, "Call if you've

found this loyal sled. Goes by name of Bud." I signed it and closed it up. John had already skied away. I turned both sleds to face north. They'd put in their time and deserved that honor.

This was a transition to an even simpler life. Now the going would be easier, there'd be no more shuttling back and forth. Once or twice I looked over my shoulder. Seeing them sitting there empty made me sad.

My thoughts turned back to the familiar rhythms of our early morning march.

DAY 35

86° 20.510' N
074° 53.601' W

NORTH POLE

Ellesmere Island

> ## "Not all those who wander are lost."
> —J.R.R. Tolkien

Victorinox sundial.

Finding a beacon.
It can be a challenge

By Tyler Fish

Our expedition map for the entire 416-nm route was about the size of a sheet of notebook paper. At some point during the second week we threw it out. We no longer needed it. Ward Hunt Island and the coastal mountains of Ellesmere, the only landforms on our whole journey, were now out of sight. As far as surface maps were concerned, the remainder of our trip would be featureless. Longitude and latitude were all we needed. For daily navigation we relied on three pieces of equipment: the DeLorme PN-40 GPS, a compass, and our Victorinox Swiss Army timepieces.

The DeLorme PN-40 GPS gave us our exact location and distances traveled. At each break we eagerly flipped it on to get the results of the previous march and the day's total distance. In addition to the time of sunrise and sunset, the PN-40 showed us the phase of the moon, which affects tides

Route check. Tyler on Day 13 with the Delorme PN-40 GPS.

and thus the movement of the pack ice. When the ice was drifting we could stand still and register our rate of drift by looking at the speed readout. It also gave us the readings we needed to set our compasses to the correct declination (the difference between the magnetic and geographic North Poles). Lastly, we used the PN-40 to digitally record the expedition's route log.

In order to travel in a straight line we simply set our compass to the correct declination and bearing as given by our GPS and then waited for the magnetic compass to point us in the right direction. Because we were so close to the Magnetic North Pole (then located near 84° N, 120° W), our compasses could take up to a minute to settle out. Once we had our bearing locked in, we looked for an ice formation on the horizon to mark our path of travel. Depending on the position and brightness of the sun and the topography of rubble, these points, or beacons as we sometimes called them, could be anywhere from two hundred yards to two miles away. Sometimes we used the angle of our shadow to guide us. To do this we faced directly toward our compass bearing and noted the angle of our shadow. Then during the march we just kept the shadow in the same relative position. We could also calculate the angle of our shadow if we knew our exact longitude.

BY GLORIA LEON, PHD.

Professor Emerita, Department of Psychology, University of Minnesota

BY JOHN HUSTON

Courtesy of Professor Gloria Leon

Professor Gloria Leon.

NASA and space agencies in other countries consider expeditions carried out in isolated and extreme environments to be an analog for space missions. Following this perspective, a group of researchers at the University of Minnesota and the University of Bergen in Norway (Gro M. Sandal, Birgit Fink, Paul Ciofani, and I) studied John and Tyler for an extended period prior to the start of their expedition until six months after the completion of the trek.

The focus of the research was on the evaluation of personality characteristics and attitudes of the two men, the way in which they interacted, the processes by which they made decisions, and the possible changes in personal attitudes and values as a result of their expedition experiences. (The research report will be published in a forthcoming edition of the scientific journal *Environment and Behavior*.) This information can be helpful in better understanding and planning for some of the personal and interpersonal situations that might occur during exploration of the surface of the moon or Mars.

John and Tyler completed personality questionnaires and other psychological measures prior to the expedition. Once a week during the expedition, the two filled out a rating form assessing mood state, stress, coping methods, and relationship/decision making processes. Interviews and several repeat measures were carried out

at the end of the expedition and at a six-month followup.

Both men had high scores on personality scales measuring well-being and social closeness, and, in general, showed positive emotional adjustment. A second measure indicated that self-direction and stimulation were strong personal values for both team members. A significant finding was how well the two men got along together on the ice. Decisions were made after considerable discussion between the two team members. Through this process, they were able to reach a consensus on strategies to successfully achieve their goal.

In addition, both men were sensitive to and respectful of each other's needs and mood states. They indicated that, basically, they took care of each other. This included sharing food and helping with loads and chores as needed. Both reported aspects of personal growth from the end of the expedition to the followup, based on their experiences during the trek. Contrary to previous studies of all-male expedition teams, John and Tyler did not exhibit strong competitiveness with each other.

The personality characteristics identified on the psychological measures and the data from the weekly ratings and later interviews provided information that could be helpful in selecting individuals for future expeditions and other missions in extreme and isolated environments.

No, but with qualifications, yes. Traditionally, the term "explorer" refers to an expedition leader who discovers places on Earth previously unknown to European society. Leif Ericson, Ferdinand Magellan, and Alexander Mackenzie were explorers. Polar explorers of the late nineteenth and early twentieth centuries—Roald Amundsen, Fridtjof Nansen, Ernest Shackleton, Robert Scott, Robert Peary, and others—led expeditions that filled in blank spaces on the globe.

The last unmapped places on Earth are on the bottom of the ocean or in undiscovered caves. Polar explorers hold on to the "explorer" moniker mainly because it's the easiest way to describe what we do. Technically, we're expeditioners. Today's polar explorers travel the Earth's coldest regions on multi-month expeditions. These expeditions may seek to establish a new route, achieve a goal via a particular travel method, or break a record. They may add small bits of information to science, but by and large, modern polar expeditions are an exploration into oneself.

8 Ten-Day Circus

By Tyler Fish

"I am a slow walker, but I never walk backwards." —Abraham Lincoln

During the previous few days the huge, looming lead near 87° N dominated our thoughts. Until we were across, our northward progress would be in doubt. If it was open, or if we encountered it in bad weather, we could be stalled for several days or even a week.

After a productive first march of 3.0 nm on Day 36, we came to a hulking ridge that had been on the horizon for a while.

"Wow, a rubble farm," I said, as I got out the video camera.

"It looks pretty new," John said. The ice here was much slipperier than on the snow-covered piles we were used to.

Glistening, foot-thick slabs formed a chaotic barricade eight feet high, running east-west. John maneuvered through the rubble first. When I caught up to him fifty yards later, he was checking the ice at the edge of a massive lead.

We could barely make out the other side. This was the big lead Julie had told us about.

As we paused, taking in what lay in front of us, I heard a strange sound.

The ice was moving! Every three seconds it gave out a grunting, squeaking sigh. The newly frozen lead was closing, a few inches at a time. The thinner ice to the north was being forced underneath the thicker ice we were standing on.

Ahead of us lay a section of dark, newly formed ice that looked skiable. Beyond that the ice looked more solid. To the west and east of us, the ice looked thinner in spots, dotted with seal-sized holes and rivulets of open water. We had hit the lead at the perfect location. This would save us hours, maybe even days.

John set forth with the safety rope trailing behind his sled, leaving moist gray tracks in the thin layer of frost flowers. The ice flexed under his weight, but it held. After seventy yards he reached a section of more solid ice and stopped. I followed, skiing alongside his tracks.

The lead looked at least a half-mile wide. Would we make it across? We feared that we'd run into weak ice in the middle, or worse, a shift in the ice pack might split the new ice into pieces. Thankfully, the wind was calm. The sky was clear blue and the whole scene was bathed in brilliant sunshine.

Soon we were gliding softly across fields of giant frost flowers, a base of solid ice beneath us.

The ice to the north looked white and solid as well. The rubble-strewn ridge

Rubble farm. Day 36, 11:50 p.m.

Mile-wide lead. Looking north, Day 36, 11:50 p.m.

Night sun. Day 38, 8:55 p.m.

to the south had faded from view, and it seemed like we could see forever in all directions.

Skiing over progressively thicker ice, with just a few cracks to step over, we finally reached the northern edge. It took us about an hour. We had counted our strides and estimated it to be at least a nautical mile across. Once back on the older ice, we took a break behind a ridge, happy to be past our scariest obstacle so far.

We spent Days 35 through 38 living life at -20° F, consistently besting the previous day's progress (8.8 nm, 9.7 nm, 11.2 nm, and 11.7 nm).

On Day 36, we boosted our rations to 7,500 calories per day. Dinners and breakfasts were appreciably bigger, and we had a few more truffles for lunch. Once we upped our travel hours again the extra food wouldn't seem like a luxury.

On the morning of Day 39, just before breakfast, John was studying the GPS when he looked up and said, "We drifted south last night."

We both knew what this meant. We were now skiing upstream.

The surface of the Arctic Ocean consists of gigantic pans of ice that move at the whims of wind and ocean currents. Until now the ice pans we traveled on had

Evening baggage. John assembles stuff sacks that enter the tent each night, Day 37.

Frost flower garden. Day 36.

Frost flowers.

been jammed into a locked position. Now the pans of ice that we stood on were drifting south.

In anticipation of the southern drift, we had worked hard to get two days ahead of schedule. At any moment the rate and direction of drift could change. Our ability to adapt to this unseen force would largely determine our success.

That day we crossed 87° N—180 nm to go. In a car on the highway we'd be there in three or four hours.

It was time to lengthen our travel day to eleven hours. We'd sleep as much as our 5:00 a.m. wakeup allowed—six to seven hours.

As we traveled, our thoughts were partly determined by which person was in front. The leader thinks about what lies ahead: Where are we going? What are the obstacles? Are there any leads? Ridges? What's the easiest path? How far is my partner behind me?

The follower is able to take a mental break. I'd lose myself thinking about the snow: Look at these rippled patterns. Here's a crusty stretch. Whoa, frost flowers everywhere.

Ski tip view. Day 39.

Two-Mile Mess. Tyler takes a seat before going up and over.

Hungry beast. John discovers a few loose spoonfuls of freeze-dried cheese in his backpack. It did not go to waste.

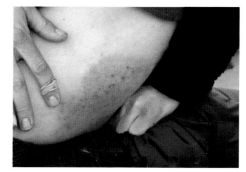

Chilblains. A form of mild frostbite on John's hip. The sores were itchy and annoying but cleared up soon after we got home.

There were daydreams of home. I imagined what my son Ethan looked like. John made plans—a surprise weekend getaway for Jennifer's birthday and a road trip to New Mexico with his brother and sister.

On breaks we talked more and more about food. At one point John said, "I wonder how long I'm going to want to eat everything I see."

The full moon arrived on the morning of Day 40. Full moons bring high tides, leading to more ice movement and open water. As we trudged along, we could see evidence of the stress. Puddles of slush and pools of water lingered in low spots on the ice.

We picked our way through a maze of frozen leads and ridges of ice, thrust up, split apart, piled together. It was like meandering for two miles along a frozen, braided river strewn with impediments. We called it the Two-Mile Mess. After that came the One-Mile Mess and the Half-Mile Mess, each a little less messy than the one before.

In the tent that night I helped John bandage the chilblains (minor frostbite) on his hips. The purplish layer of frozen skin had turned into a weeping sore that was on its way to drying out. I had them in the same spot, but mine weren't as bad. They weren't that painful, just itchy.

Aside from this minor injury, our health was better than we could have hoped. I had a little superficial frostbite on my nose. Our legs were skinnier. In the tent I kept getting upper leg cramps, which were annoying but not debilitating. We had no muscle or joint aches at all and our feet were in great shape. The washings and extra attention we gave them were paying off. Happy dogs make happy skiers.

Good thoughts today about our consistent travel and brother-like relationship. Could be having more fun. But we care a lot for each other and are totally a team. The fun is just not there and I don't know why.

At the end of Day 41 John told me he'd been in a funk for the past few days. He was focusing too much on what we called the Uncontrollables: the drift, the weather, the April 26 deadline. We were trying not to dwell on aspects of the expedition that we couldn't influence, but with only two weeks to go, our thoughts had begun to wander to the finish line. The pressure was building.

That night we drifted almost 2.0 nm to the southeast. There was little we could do. It was too early for a big push. We'd never recover. So we decided to ski a little to the northwest.

Recently we'd come up with a new way of entertaining ourselves during the day. I'd ask John a question. He'd give me a preliminary answer. Then we'd be off skiing. When we met up again he'd have a more complete response. Then he might ask me a question and we'd continue on. It could take up to forty-five minutes before I had a chance to answer him. Our topics ranged all over the place, from gear, to random trivia, to fatherhood.

These conversations also helped us assess our tactics. Both of us had strong thoughts about what to do next. I tended to react quickly to John's ideas, and I felt he often dismissed mine. It wasn't good, but it was the pattern we'd fallen into even

before the expedition began. The delays built into this ongoing ramble gave us time to weigh each other's proposals.

Around 4:00 p.m. on Day 43 we came to an open lead running east-west. If we skied along the lead, it might be a long time before we found a place to cross. I was confident we could swim it.

John was less certain, but he agreed to give it a shot. For the first time on the expedition we pulled the big orange drysuits out of their stuff sacks. John put his on with some effort, but mine wouldn't go on. I couldn't get my boots into the feet of the suit.

I was mad. Once again, the last-minute boot decision in Iqaluit was affecting me. I decided to swim in my boot liners. But now I couldn't get my hands into the arms of the suit without taking off my thick mittens. I would only be wearing thin liner mittens.

It took us an hour to get ready. We spent part of that time hopping around and whirling our arms to ward off the cold. We should have eaten something by now, but I just wanted to swim.

We made our way to the edge. John looked at me. "We don't have to do this. Maybe we should just stop the train."

Cramp avoidance. Tyler stretches out. Leg cramps plagued him much of the way.

Rest stop. On breaks we always tried to get off our feet.

Distance gauge. How far away is that snow mound? The light constantly played tricks on our depth perception.

He was right. This moment had all the makings of an accident waiting to happen. It was almost time to stop for the day, anyway. We decided to cut our losses and camp on the south side of the lead.

We'd only netted 8.4 nm in ten and a half hours. We had twelve days left and almost 140 nautical miles to go. Each mile that we failed to gain in a given day added to the average distance we'd have to cover in the remaining days. The drift compounded the problem. We were constantly turning this calculation over in our heads.

If our egos were damaged by the aborted swim, the ocean rubbed our noses in it the next morning. The lead had grown. It was now at least two hundred yards wide. And we'd drifted almost three nm east-southeast during the night.

We skied west along the lead and came to a place where it narrowed into a collection of ice chunks, basketball-sized popcorn, and slush. Even though we didn't have to swim, we chose to try again anyway. The day was young, and we needed to get this right.

As I was pulling out my drysuit, I heard voices. We looked west. I didn't have my glasses on, but I was reasonably sure that two people were skiing toward us along the lead, yelling.

The bigger of the two men shouted, "You guys are doing awesome!" They knew who we were, but we didn't know of any teams that could be near us. Soon we were

Two weeks to go. John alone with his thoughts. Tyler alone with his, Day 41.

sharing stories with Keith Heger and Sebastian Copeland, a guide and client duo who had begun their expedition at 85° N. Keith was also from Chicago and had met John a few years earlier.

It was fun—and funny—to suddenly interact with other humans in this faraway place, where running into a polar bear would've been more likely. John made Keith's day with news of a big Chicago Bears trade and detailed plans for consuming mass quantities of deep-dish pizza when he got back home.

They were already "rolling the clock," working extended days so that a "day" was more than twenty-four hours long. We were beginning our day, they were ending theirs. After swapping stories and snapping a few pictures, we parted ways. They scampered across the icy mess without putting on drysuits, and we proceeded with our plan to swim, eager to put last night's hassles behind us.

I expected that getting into my drysuit would be an ordeal, but I noticed that John's went on much easier this time. With little effort, I pulled mine on. We guessed that the suits had loosened up after being released from forty days of compressed storage.

Fully suited, John was walking in front of his sled near the edge of the lead when he suddenly broke through. There he was, bobbing in the slushy water and laughing. He hauled himself onto a large floating chunk a few yards away and pulled the sled up after him. I followed. We were two fat orange frogs swimming from one lily pad to the next.

A few minutes later we reached a stretch of weak-looking ice—dark, with small frost flowers just beginning to form. This section separated us from the northern edge of the lead. We kept our drysuits on and walked across. The ice bowed and flexed underneath us but didn't tear. On the other side we shed our drysuits and clipped into our skis.

It wasn't too long before we caught and passed the other team. They camped soon thereafter and we didn't see them again.

The next day, Day 45, we increased our travel time from eleven to thirteen hours to build a bigger cushion. The extra two hours of travel would cut our sleep to five hours a night.

I worked hard to stay focused and awake during the last two hours of that first thirteen-hour day. John seemed to be going pretty strong, as was his habit at the end of the day. "I'll feel better tomorrow," I told myself. It was just the typical shock to

Icestache. Tyler, Day 41.

Phoning home. John calls in a blog entry.

Morning sublimation. John hangs up sleeping bags at 6:26 a.m. A daily routine during the sunny days of April. Ice that had built up in the down insulation vanished after exposure to direct sunlight.

the system that goes with a change in routine.

That day we found ourselves drifting directly south. But we managed to cross our next line of latitude anyway. "Eighty-eight degrees, baby!" John shouted as we sat together during a break, sheltered from the wind.

"Mmmm," was my enthusiastic response as I spooned butter, bacon, and nuts out of my lunch bag and into my mouth. It had taken us forty-five days and a whole lot of snack breaks to get here.

"I'm dialing in for the final push," John said. "Those last few days, we're gonna be tired. Big time. We can't let it matter, though."

I nodded. I didn't want to think about it too much until I had to.

"But we won't be tired at the end," he went on. "We'll be so energized by getting there."

"And then?"

"We'll feel really tired."

The wind was whipping steadily again. John chewed contentedly on a white chocolate truffle. I was trying to cram a truffle into my mouth, but the icicle built up on my mustache was in the way. The icicle came off with a painful brush of my mitten.

That day we made 14.5 nm, another best.

It was my wife's birthday. I'd been composing a song for her, a mashup of a few different songs with my own lyrics added. She wasn't home when I called, so I sang into the answering machine.

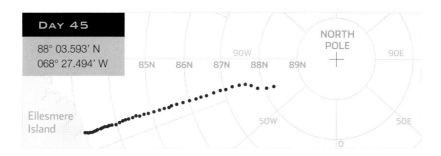

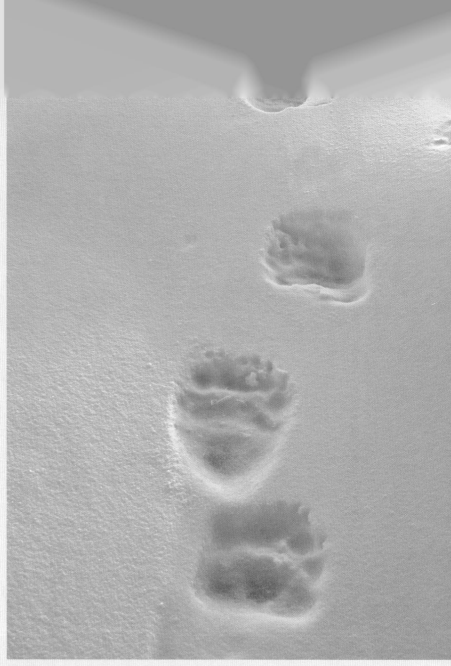

By John Huston

There's no doubt that skiing unsupported to the North Pole from Canada is one of the wildest trips on the planet, but it's not because of the wildlife.

Our route, historically, is somewhat devoid of animal encounters. This held true for our expedition. We considered that a very good thing, because on the Arctic Ocean all animal life is polar bear food, including humans. The more animals we saw, the greater our chance of encountering bears. In this anthropocentric world, where we are distanced from our food sources, it's a rare and humbling thing not to be at the top of the food chain.

Polar bears are the undisputed kings of the Arctic. Males can reach 7.9 feet in height and can weigh fifteen hundred pounds. These killing machines can pick up a scent thirty miles away, run up to twenty-five miles per hour and swim up to six miles per hour. They travel vast distances in search of food, mates, and dens. Seals are their favorite food, so bears congregate near areas of thin ice and open water. We expected the chance of an encounter to decrease as we moved north, but polar bears have been spotted as far north as the Pole itself.

Fortunately for us, the dense pack ice off Ward Hunt Island contains very little open water and supports little in the way of animal life in early March. However, we carried a Winchester 12-gauge marine grade shotgun for bear protection. Shotguns are standard safety equipment when traveling in the Arctic. They are used only in emergencies and most commonly as noisemakers. Tyler trained with our shotgun for several months. He slept with the gun next to him in the tent each night.

Besides ice bears, as Norwegians call them, we knew we might encounter Arctic foxes and seals. Arctic foxes are wide-ranging scavengers. During Arctic Ocean winters they mostly feed off the remains of polar bear kills. Seals swim beneath the sea ice and frequently pop their heads out of open or freshly frozen leads.

Big mama. Fairly fresh tracks, Day 20. At least eight inches wide and twelve inches long.

Bear signs, Day 9. The tracks and the scat look like they've been there quite a while.

Seal lead, Day 30. Ten minutes after we took this photo, a seal popped its head out of the middle of the lead.

Fox tracks, Day 31. An Arctic Fox tested this lead before we did.

Cubs, Day 20. Tracks from two bear cubs walking behind their mother.

WILDLIFE ENCOUNTERS

Day 9: Polar bear tracks and scat. The tracks ran from west to east and appeared to be several weeks old.

Day 20: Polar bear tracks. They appeared to be less than forty-eight hours old, as identified by a lack of snow cover in the tracks. The tracks were from a mother and two cubs, traveling from north to south. This encounter put us on alert.

Day 30: Seals. We saw one or two seals pop their heads out of a freshly frozen lead. Tyler was filming me at the time and we caught it on video.

Entire expedition: Arctic fox tracks. We saw meandering trails all along our route, even north of 88° 30' N.

BY JOHN HUSTON

Using drysuits to swim across leads gave us peace of mind and a significant margin of safety.

The water we swam in was around 30° F. The air temperature was normally -10° F or colder. This meant that the water was at least 40° F warmer than the air.

Most people see photos of us swimming in the Arctic Ocean and gasp, "I could never do that." Even after we explain that it's a relatively warm experience and that our cold hands actually warm up as soon as we hit the water, most people still don't get it. The concept is too far out there. However, because water conducts heat away from the body twenty-five times faster than air of the same temperature, swimming does feel colder the longer you are in the water.

Ever since the first explorers set out for the North Pole, crossing leads has presented a difficult puzzle. Some used a boat, but boats come with major drawbacks. Wooden boats are heavy and easily damaged by rubble and the extreme cold. Inflatable boats are easily punctured. Some explorers paddle their sleds across leads, but this can require a time-intensive repacking of gear.

In the early 1990s Børge Ousland pioneered the use of drysuits to cross leads. These suits are waterproof, lightweight, easy to use, and surprisingly tough to puncture. You slip the suit over your boots and outer layers, zip it up, and slide on your butt into the water. The suits trap air, so you're quite buoyant in the water.

1

No way over or around. Time to swim.

2

The dry suit goes on.

3

Tyler first. A rope is clipped to his foot. Swimming isn't as cold as it looks. The water is at least 40° F warmer than the air.

4

Tyler on the other side. He pulls the sleds across with the rope.

5

John's turn. Sliding into the water.

6

Turning to head across. Note the air trapped in the legs of his suit.

7

Approaching the other side.

8

Getting out. It can be tricky.

9

A roll in the snow. The snow soaks up water, allowing the suit to be dusted off.

10

On skis again. Total elapsed time: 25-45 minutes.

9 RANT AND RESCUE

BY TYLER FISH

DAYS 46–47: APRIL 16–17, 2009

"If you are going through hell, keep going." —Winston Churchill

Day 46 didn't dawn. The sun was still up from the day before. That evening we sat in the comfortably warm tent. During his blog dictation, John took a stab at answering the question "How hard is this expedition?" He did a nice job of it: "Suffice it to say that this is one of the most difficult, all-encompassing challenges that we've ever undertaken. We feel good about how we're going about it and that makes it feel a lot less difficult."

That same night I went to lie down before dinner and a cramp hit my upper right thigh. I groaned and tried to straighten my leg, massaging the knot till it gradually went away. I wished we had brought more salt, which would have helped balance my electrolytes. These leg cramps were hitting me more often now, almost like they were stalking me. I'd feel the muscles threatening to spasm, but most of the time I could prevent it.

I did my stretching while John melted snow and cooked dinner. This was one of the few times of the day when I could truly relax. We were alone a lot during the day, but this was different. I needed the downtime to think.

Over the past few days I'd been feeling more and more agitated, storing up guilt about some of our interactions. I'd been a little snappy in ways that John didn't deserve, and that evening, in response to one of my remarks, he asked me what was behind it. I owed him an explanation, but we were dog-tired and it was nearing bedtime. I needed to think about what to say. We agreed to talk in the morning.

What's causing me to be short and rude with him at times? I feel he is controlling, but why does he need to be? How much of this comes from my own personal issues? How much is he aware of my feelings? How can we move past this? I'd pondered these topics, but I could only delve so deep before being distracted by cold hands or some other detail.

There was too much between us that had gone unsaid for a long time. I had opinions about us that I'd never shared. Much of this didn't matter now, except that it added to the tension. I think I just wanted John to understand me more, to really get where I was coming from. If that were possible, then I could free myself of some of my guilt, and he wouldn't feel like my reactions were his fault.

As I fell asleep I went over what I would say. It would come as a surprise to him, and it would be hard for him to hear it all. I hadn't intended to save it all up.

The next morning John and I sat in the diffuse morning light of the tent. The stoves warmed the kettle with a muffled roar. It was a good time to talk.

I had a lot to unload, so this would be more of a monologue than a conversation.

Along a lead. Tyler, Day 46, 6:39 p.m.

Day 46, 9:51 p.m. Tyler unloads his pulk.

I didn't expect John to say much, I just needed to get it all out.

"I need to explain why I've been so snappy and curt. You deserve to hear it. I don't want this affecting us anymore."

John sat there taking in my words.

"First of all, I feel that you don't show enough respect for my outdoor knowledge, or my career for that matter.

"Think about it. At Outward Bound I was one of your supervisors. Now we've flipped the balance of power. That's been tough for me.

"And I was really jealous of your Greenland expedition. To me it didn't seem fair that a younger guy would get that opportunity and not me.

"I was pumped about teaming up with you for the North Pole, but it's been a constant struggle. Our partnership has been unequal and it's hurt us on the ice."

John listened, sometimes looking at me, sometimes staring at something else. I did the same.

I went on to describe my frustration with the planning and fundraising, and how we failed to make good use of my

Crowded cortex. John during the first march of Day 47.

strengths and skills. I told him about sharing my complaints with Sarah and how she said, "Someone's got to lead the fundraising, and it's good that it's John." I told him what a relief that was but that I still felt I wasn't contributing, and that the times when I did accomplish something, we didn't follow up, so I felt like I was busting my ass for nothing.

"I feel bad about holding all this in."

I didn't want to overload him. That wouldn't be fair, but neither would an incomplete message.

"I got tired of your suggestions. I didn't want you telling me what to do. I'm the type that needs to experience things for myself.

"I wanted to contribute equally. But my time constraints and our awkward dynamic got in the way. The guilt has been killing my spirit." I paused. "I should've said something a long time ago, but since you were doing so much of the work, I didn't feel it was my place. So I tried to bury it."

The light in the tent had grown brighter. Breakfast was finished. John asked a few fair questions but didn't have much to say.

"I'm glad you shared all that." I could tell he just wanted to take it and ski on it.

In no time the tent was down. Pulks were packed. We were ready to ski.

A burden had been lifted, but questions surrounded me like thick air. Why had I held on to all of this? How was John doing? We had discussed our partnership a few times over the past three years, but it had been too long.

After I watched him ski away, I leaned on my poles and looked down. The best people in my life are the ones I've walked through fire with. We always came out on the other side stronger for it.

I skied through that first march in a cloud of emotions. It seemed like the next time I looked up I saw gray ice. John was ahead of me, standing at the edge of a newly frozen lead. From where I stood it looked skiable.

"It looks like the same ice we skied over yesterday," I yelled to him over the wind. "It looks good."

John stabbed at the ice a few times and skied onto the lead, slowly.

He skied over a little crack, his pulk sliding behind him onto the new ice. Then I saw it. The ice was softening,

Frozen remnants. Thirty minutes after the rescue. The tent is forty yards away.

sucking at the back of his skis. "You're going through! Ski!"

What was going on? This couldn't happen. No way. I stood there, waiting, watching, swearing. With each stride he sank deeper and deeper.

I unclipped my pulk, grabbed the throw bag, and skied toward the edge. This had to work.

But it didn't. The bag fell short, tangled. I didn't bother trying again. John was up to his neck, ski-swimming toward me. "Keep those skis on!"

Icy patch. Post dunking.

I extended a pole, kneeling at the edge. Years of lifeguarding mantras rang in my head. "Reach, throw, don't go." I couldn't fall in. That would be disaster. It might even mean death.

The ice began to crack beneath me. Water pooled around my knees. "Be smart," I thought. I slid backward to more solid ice and stood up. Nearing the edge John tossed his ski poles at my feet.

He was trying to clamber up, but the ice kept breaking away. Finally it held and he hauled himself out. "Pole!" he yelled. I handed him my pole as he got to his feet. Planting the pole he dragged the pulk out of the water and skied another twenty yards away from the edge.

"Clothes!" he bellowed. I was already rifling through his pulk, searching for his clothing stuff sack.

There wasn't much time. Soon his hands would be too cold to use. Frostbite would be next. He removed his backpack, untied his boots, and started yelling for different articles of clothing. He was desperate, but I couldn't be. We could do this. We'd done it before, just never for real.

I put a sleeping pad down on the snow for him to stand on. He began peeling off his clothes.

More yelling. He was in pain, near panic, it seemed. John always got loud when he was cold, but this was new territory.

John was now struggling to get his long underwear shirt over his head. We suddenly realized that his watch, worn over the wrist of his shirt, was clamping the soaked garment to his arm. He pulled the shirt back down but couldn't get the watch off.

With bare fingers I got it loose. But it hurt. I knew right away I'd frozen the tip of my thumb on the metal clasp.

John put on a dry shirt and long underwear bottoms. I helped with the other layers as his hands clenched with cold. He shoved them into his armpits.

John slid into a sleeping bag and sat there rocking, trying to warm up. I wrapped another bag around him and fed him a few truffles. Somehow he'd managed to keep his sunglasses and wool hat on the whole time!

I stood next to him for a moment. His hands were slightly better but his feet were still numb. He would recover, but it would be slow. I only hoped there'd been no damage to his extremities.

I found a place to set up the tent forty yards to the south.

Once we were in the tent, I fired up the stoves. Within minutes everything smelled like soggy dog. It looked like a bucket of slush had spilled on the floor.

I headed out to take pictures and grab the frozen blobs of clothing. How much time would this stuff take to dry? How much fuel would it take? We didn't have enough of either.

I stood there for a moment outside the tent. The stoves roared away inside. This

Rough recovery. John readies himself to start skiing again.

was our fault.

Inside, John's long underwear, mittens, and boot liners hung from the drying lines. His sopping boots lay on the floor. It would take hours to dry everything, but we couldn't wait for that. We had to keep moving.

I didn't need the truffles I'd been saving, and I could live without one layer of underwear and my extra mitten liners. I handed these over to my friend. He looked stunned—weary, pale, and diminished.

Eventually John asked the inevitable. "What do you think we should do?"

"I think we have to keep going."

"Yeah." He was resigned to it.

Dry layers close to skin. Wet layers next. Fleece pants and jacket on top. John would ski and be damp, but warm.

Soon enough we were on our way, headed west along the lead. I skied in front, looking for a safe place to cross.

An hour later I spotted a small span of whiter ice zigzagging its way across the lead. Would it hold? I tested it with my ski pole. So far so good. I considered the safer options: putting on drysuits or waiting for better ice.

No. We needed to regain our confidence. I skied out onto the lead. John waited.

I reached the first corner of the zigzag. The ice was looking and feeling stronger. "I think we're good, John."

We shuffled our way to the other side where we high-fived with sweet relief. We would end this day well.

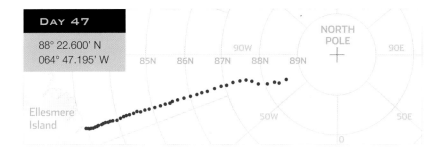

10 UPSTREAM

BY JOHN HUSTON

"No pressure, no diamonds." —Thomas Carlyle

After I fell through the ice, it took me at least three days to recover. We were faced with the dismal task of drying out my wet clothes while burning as little fuel as possible. Over the past month we had battled to save fuel. Thanks mainly to warmer temperatures we had built up a small reserve. Now, due to the ninety-minute dryout after my dunking, we were back on the edge.

We hung up one or two items at a time in the cone of the tent while the stoves were lit for cooking. The dripping made a salty puddle of grime and slush on the floor of the tent. You know you have a true friend when he doesn't hesitate to wring out the socks and long underwear you've worn for thirty days straight.

Dealing with the aftermath of the dunking wasn't our only problem. The drift was accelerating. We were near the Lomonosov Ridge, an underwater geological feature that rises to 12,000 feet above the sea floor. This ridge bisects the Arctic Ocean, contributing to a strong ocean current that was now pushing us east and south.

When we crossed 88° N on Day 44, we were two days ahead of schedule. Now our cushion was eroding. If the drift didn't slow down, we'd soon be in trouble. This realization weighed on us as we clipped into our bindings and headed out to start Day 48.

The wind had blown ceaselessly during the night. Once out from behind the rubbled lee of the campsite, I encountered a stretch of new six-inch drifts. If our forecast for more wind and blowing snow held true, these growing drifts would kill our pace.

We meandered through crazy weather all day. The wind continued to batter us. Light conditions ranged from sunny to near-whiteout, shifting every few hours. Our perceived temperature varied from too warm to frigid, as the sun appeared and disappeared behind low-lying clouds.

The strange light toyed with our depth perception. We could make out blue ice chunks a hundred yards away but stumbled blindly into fresh snowdrifts right in front of us. Sometimes we'd think an ice chunk was two hundred yards away, only to ski up to it five strides later.

On some breaks I began to shiver within minutes of stopping. My body had consumed all of its insulating fat reserves. Right after the dunking, I'd scarfed down more than my daily ration of nuts and truffles. Now, I was paying for it. I had to

Blue ridge in whiteout. Afternoon, Day 48.

subsist on less until we opened the next five-day rotation of food. Tyler must have sensed me staring into his lunch bag. He gave me a few more of the truffles he'd been saving up. I thanked him with the gratitude of a truly hungry man.

A lot had happened since Tyler's rant yesterday. It now seemed like a long time ago. Although the episode hadn't been fully resolved, I was too consumed with the weather, the drift, and the dunking to think it through.

Now, anytime we stopped we were moving away from the Pole. Several times I measured drift rates of 0.3 or 0.4 nautical miles per hour (nmph). Anything over 0.2 nmph worried us. Over the course of a twenty-four-hour day, 0.25 nmph would

Nackered. Tyler, Day 48, 9:15 p.m.

amount to 6.0 nm of drift. If most of that drift was southward, then almost half of our northward distance would be canceled out.

On the evening of Day 48 I called Julie for the weekly check-in. She'd been in contact with Victor Boyarsky, who ran Barneo, the Russian base located near the Pole. She confirmed that Barneo was still scheduled to leave the ice on April 26. This gave us eight days to ski the remaining eighty-seven miles. In spite of the drift, Tyler and I felt we could average the 11 nm a day needed to reach the Pole in time for the last flight out. A mishap or weather delay would hurt our chances.

TYLER'S BLOG ENTRY / DAY 48

What is going to get us to the North Pole? I think we both realize that it's hard work, patience, and care for each other. Those are the three things that are going to get us there, and we just have to do them every day.

The next morning we woke up 3.3 nm east-southeast of where we fell asleep. After hammering the tent all night, the wind now blew even harder, and low-hanging clouds cut visibility to practically zero.

It was Sunday. We made our Family Day phone calls before breaking camp. This time the conversations focused on the logistics of our arrival in Norway, little more than a week away. During the past two weeks while skiing, I'd envisioned the reunion at the airport over and over, hugging Jennifer and eating the chocolate cake that Tyler and I had requested.

Our Family Day conversations helped sustain us as we stumbled through the whiteout, but worries about the narrowing time window soon took over. Over the previous few days we'd hashed out a plan for rolling the clock—switching to a twenty-seven-hour clock instead of the standard twenty-four hours. It hadn't been dark for two weeks now. We could ski for seventeen hours and use the rest of the time to sleep and eat. We had to be careful, though. If we began rolling the clock too early we risked exhausting ourselves, preventing a final all-out dash to the Pole.

On the morning of Day 49 that final dash seemed a long way off. The whiteout and wind persisted, and so did the southward drift. The snowdrifts had tripled in size. These conditions were sure to slow us down. All morning long I crunched the numbers, working through the amount of time remaining, rate of drift, distances,

Toward the light. Evening, Day 48.

Rubble way. Sometimes it's the only way. Day 49.

Typical view. Taking a break, Day 50, 10:04 p.m.

Wearing down. Wind, snow, and rubble take a toll. John, early evening, Day 49.

hours of sleep, and alternate travel schedules.

During a midday break, we leaned against a small ridge and put our feet up on my sled, enjoying a respite from the wind.

"I've been doing calculations in my head all morning," Tyler said.

"Yeah," I said. "Me too. Slow calculations. My brain is a snail."

"We can only assume this wind will get worse," Tyler said. "I think we should roll the clock."

"I agree."

We decided on a 27-hour day: 16.5 hours of travel, 2 hours to set up camp and eat dinner, 6 hours of sleep, and then 2.5 hours for breakfast, water, and breaking down camp. The plan would give us a most welcome extra hour of sleep.

Tyler and I had been getting along better since he unloaded his frustrations two days earlier. Although I'd felt blindsided, I knew it was healthy for him to release those feelings. The problem was, I could tell Tyler was still feeling guilty. I wondered what I should do. Worrying about the past as we pushed to the brink of exhaustion would kill us.

During a march that afternoon we stood next to each other as I struggled to find a compass bearing. Searching for a landmark in a sea of white upon white, I

Into the midnight sun.

found a bluish blob in the distance. I skied a few steps and then turned back to Tyler. It was my turn to clear the air.

"I've been thinking about what you said, about not helping enough with the preparation. I forgive you for that." I reached over and gave him a hug.

"Thanks," he said. There were tears in his eyes.

An hour later, Tyler told me that my forgiveness meant a lot to him. I was glad to hear it. The coming days would require every ounce of our energy.

As I skied along that afternoon I realized that we'd been through something important, and painfully human. I thought of us as two siblings ashamed of letting a squabble get out of hand. We were ready to move on with a new understanding.

In the late evening the whiteout finally broke. The sun floated through its nighttime track, silhouetting the distant ice chunks. I homed in on a piece of elevated rubble. When we reached this beacon three hours later, it was time to camp.

Day 49 netted us 15.5 nm, despite the drift. Our route crossed several open or

Heavy discussion. Deciding to roll the clock, Day 49, 4:14 p.m.

newly frozen leads, two of which we swam. The ice pack was loosening. We pitched our tent just south of a ten-foot-high ridge that ran east-west.

We fell asleep 12.0 nm short of 89° N, hoping that a good day tomorrow would put us past this last parallel for good. During the night we heard a cracking of the ice somewhere close, but not close enough to worry about.

When we woke up the sun was shining brightly for the first morning in several days. Our GPS read 88° 45' N—3.0 nm south of our position the night before. Tyler and I were in high spirits as we packed our sleds, confident that our new plan would get us to the Pole.

I led out of camp and made my way over the ridge. Eighty feet later I stopped. "Wooof!" A three-foot-wide crack running parallel to the ridge had opened up overnight. That was the noise that had woken us. "Did we camp on the right side of the ridge or what?"

"I can't believe it," Tyler said. "I think we still would've been safe, though. We were close enough to the ridge." The ice there would have been the strongest. We jumped across the crack and continued skiing north.

Halfway through the day our friend, the whiteout, was back. The wind increased from ten to twenty knots, and the snowdrifts started to firm up.

The rate of firming up depends on wind speed. A really big blow can turn loose drifts into hard packed snow overnight. With a lesser wind it can take days. Until the drifts firm up completely, it feels like you're pulling sleds through wet concrete.

We'd begun our travel day at 2:12 a.m. on April 20, and planned to stop at 6:45 p.m. that evening. Tyler struggled through the nighttime hours, but he never complained about it. Sometimes he took a five-minute nap during breaks. I ended up leading more marches to give him a breather. I didn't mind at all; he'd picked me up several times thus far. It was like we had an unstated mantra to do the little things that made the other person's life easier.

The sticky drifts and near-zero visibility made the last few marches of the day miserable. We decided to camp early. Our pace was so slow that an extra hour of skiing wouldn't be worth it.

We struggled mightily to erect the tent on snow that was too soft to hold the stakes. Wind howled through the lines and snow streamed around the meager ice block we had found for shelter. Worse, we couldn't find the Magic Piece, the eight-inch pole extender that supported the center of our tent. Tyler and I had fashioned

Nice form. Tyler, Day 51, 8:41 p.m.

it from an old ski pole back in Resolute.

Tyler anguished over the loss. To him the Magic Piece represented everything we had done well—our resourcefulness and attention to detail. I was bummed, too. It was my job to pack it every morning.

Again we had to improvise. We poured the last two ounces of our Scotch into an empty spice container and used the plastic bottle as a pole extender. The empty Scotch bottle actually worked better. We never did find the Magic Piece.

We had traveled 15.0 nm in fifteen and a half grueling hours. We now lay right on 89° N. Knowing the drift would take us well south of that line during six hours of sleep, we postponed our degree celebration. A degree of latitude wasn't crossed until we crossed it for good.

That night was our lowest point thus far. The weather was pounding us, we'd lost the Magic Piece, we were foggy with sleep deprivation, and we had no idea how to overcome the drift. We couldn't wait to get to sleep and start with a clean slate the next day.

There are states of existence beyond being tired. We were in one of those now.

Plugged in. Once in a while, Tyler liked to listen to a song or two in the tent.

Sleep for us had become a sort of escapist drug. We treasured every moment of it, knowing that we'd have even less in the near future.

The next morning I called Julie. The latest news wasn't good. She told us that Barneo now wanted to pull out on April 25, no later than midnight Svalbard time (5:00 p.m. our time). Our time window had just been reduced by twenty hours or more.

It was 5:00 p.m. on April 21 (Day 50). Tyler and I looked at each other blankly. We'd now have to cover more than 64.0 nm in four days while overcoming a southward drift of 6.0 nm per twenty-four hours.

"Let's just ski on it," I shrugged. "We'll figure it out. I want to get out of this nasty campsite."

Hazy horizon. Tyler out in front, Day 51.

"I agree," Tyler said. "I'm tired of all these calculations. I just want to ski. It's the only thing we can control anyway." We left camp at 5:42 p.m. on April 21, aiming to stop at 10:15 a.m. the following day.

During the first march, visibility improved, but my mood kept getting worse. My iPod was playing a tragedy-strewn podcast of *This American Life*. I had a headache and my sled seemed extra heavy. I found myself cussing at the unending obstacle course of sticky snowdrifts, three and four feet high. At our current pace we'd never make it.

Two hours later I slumped down into a wind-carved gully for the first break of the day. Tyler hopped in next to me. "We're screwed," I told him. "I don't see how we can do it." He handed me a truffle and pointed out that we had skied 2.2 nm in the first march, a good pace for these conditions. I drank a full bottle of water and swallowed two Excedrin.

I tried to bring up the schedule but Tyler told me to shut up about it and just ski. It would be better to discuss it later when our heads were clearer. "Okay," I said.

"We'll figure it out."

Rubble and snowdrifts made for tough going. Visibility came and went. Two marches later we arrived at an open lead ten yards across. We followed the lead for fifteen minutes, but it headed off to the east, so we looked for a place to swim.

I couldn't get the shrinking time window out of my head. As we snacked and put on our drysuits I raised the issue again.

"Look, Fish, I know you're fed up with the calculations and everything, but we need to make some major changes soon. If we don't, we're not going to make it!" It was early morning on April 22, and we were only at 89° 05' N. "We have to be at the Pole by 5:00 p.m. on the twenty-fifth. That's only eighty-five hours from now."

Tyler gave me a resigned look.

"Rolling the clock isn't enough," I continued. "We need a pedal-to-the-metal push."

"I know. We're only averaging one nautical mile per hour. The drift is killing us."

"We're exhausted. And we're really thin. I looked at you this morning in the

Slushy exit. John, Day 52, 3:03 a.m.

tent. Your face, your whole frame, looked gaunt. And it hit me, 'Wow, we're really in it! Look at my friend all emaciated.'"

"You look the same," he said.

"As a last resort, we can just ski and not sleep, only put up the tent to melt water and cook meals. Rune and Torry did it. It's desperate, but it's an option."

"Let's finish the travel day, put up the tent, and have a meal. We can make all the changes after that."

"Yes. We should get Julie to call Richard for advice. Then we can throw out a bunch of stuff and come up with a plan."

We swam the lead without incident. Poor visibility and rubble slowed our progress the rest of the day. By the time we stopped to camp at 9:45 a.m. on April

22, visibility was again near zero. The wind, which had been relentless over the past week, had bumped up a few more knots. Our forecast promised more of the same. We put up the tent in the sparse lee of an old hummocked ridge.

As we slurped our pemmican stew, the conversation grew circular and despondent. We were completely played out. In the past three and a half weeks we hadn't slept more than six hours a night, most nights less than five. For Tyler, sleep deprivation was a walking nightmare. My big challenge was hunger. I felt like my stomach had started to eat my body from the inside out.

For the first time, we considered the real possibility of failure. We'd been so optimistically dialed in that quitting never once crossed our minds. Now, all the positive energy was draining away. It wasn't that we didn't believe in ourselves. It was just that, staring at the deadline in our current state, we felt defeated. Images of the sponsors, family members, friends, and schoolchildren following the expedition flitted through my mind.

I laid out the problem. "We've got to factor in the drift, at least six nautical miles south every twenty-four hours. If we add the twelve to eighteen miles of drift south to the fifty-five miles between us and the Pole, we'll need to cover seventy to seventy-five miles in the next eighty hours."

"Ugh. That's not good. I can't believe they changed the date."

I sat there cursing. "I don't see how we can make it."

"I'm thinking exactly the same thing," Tyler said. "I don't want to, but I am."

Pedal to the Metal

By John Huston   Days 52–54: April 22–24, 2009

"You can always be more tired." —Kari Poppis Suomela

wanted to curl up into a ball, fall asleep, and wake up in my bed at home. How would I explain our failure to everyone?

It was my night to call in the blog. I stumbled over my words as I tried to explain that we weren't going to make it. I tried several times, but I couldn't get the words out. Tyler told me to wait till after we slept. He called Julie. While they were talking, I contemplated eating all my truffles at once. If we were going to fail, I might as well fail on a full stomach.

Tyler's conversation with Julie was short. She would call Victor at Barneo for an update, then she'd call Richard for advice.

"She was really calm and supportive. She told us to stop thinking and just go to bed for six hours. She'll help us make a new plan when we wake up." He paused. "I think she's right. We're totally unproductive right now."

We woke up six hours later with the wind tearing at the tent walls. The GPS registered a steady 0.3 nmph drift to the south-southeast. We had drifted another 2.0 nm to the south

Hopeless. John tries to dictate the blog after Day 51, April 22, 10:53 a.m.

as we slept. I went outside for the usual purpose and found myself leaning into the wind. Gusts had to be reaching twenty-five to twenty-eight knots.

Back in the tent I called Julie. In a hopeless tone I told her about the weather and the drift. "I don't think you're done yet," she said. "You still have a good shot."

"Did you speak to Richard and Victor?" I asked.

"Yes, good news from both. Victor says that the last few adventure tourist groups will be picked up by the same helicopter as you. The pickup is scheduled for 2:00 a.m., April 26, your time. I can tell Victor likes you guys. He'll do what he can."

"That's really good to hear." The new pickup date pushed back our deadline another nine hours.

"Richard was encouraging," Julie went on. "He said—and I quote—'Dump absolutely all weight but the barest essentials. Nothing in your sled is worth $150,000.'"

I laughed. That's what we'd have to pay for a Twin Otter to fly from Resolute to pick us up at the Pole. We didn't have the funds for that and never considered it an option.

Too much wind. Means too much drift.   135

Final purge. John steps into his bindings, Day 52, 11:09 p.m. The big push is ahead. Extra weight lies scattered on the snow.

New day, new outlook. We are pumped for the push, Day 52.

Julie continued, "Richard says he's fought the same kind of drift several times. He acknowledges that it's really bad, but he believes you can do it."

She outlined Richard's plan: Ski twelve hours, put up the tent, eat a meal, nap for one hour, pack up, start another twelve hours of skiing and continue this pattern all the way to the Pole. He said we should spend twelve hours traveling and three hours in the tent each rotation. He also advised us to eat as much as possible and not save any food. Eating a lot would reduce our sled weight and supply us with energy. If we were really feeling tired on the march we could take twenty-minute naps behind the sled and then continue. He cautioned us not to put too much stock in weather forecasts. We should just keep skiing and give it a shot.

Julie had been following the guided expeditions that were closing in on the Pole. All of them were significantly east of us, and their rates of drift were steeper than ours. She advised sticking with our bearing of 15° to the west of north.

We ate breakfast with renewed optimism. Tyler was excited to jettison weight. He agreed that drastic times call for drastic measures. We proceeded to ruthlessly assess every single item in our sled, right down to the pills in our medical kit.

An hour later we had piled up thirty pounds of nonessentials. This included our HP iPaq and the temperamental Solara tracking device we purchased from Aziz for $1,200. I was so happy to toss the iPaq. Not only had it been a huge pain in the ass, to me it was a ball-and-chain of emails and computers that had followed us onto the ice. We also tossed our Crazy Creek chairs and Therm-a-Rest sleeping pads, an extra stove, the covers and most of the unused pages of our journals, most of the medical kit and most of the repair kit, along with any clothing we weren't wearing. We debated tossing the video camera but thought better of it.

Although we'd done several purges earlier in the expedition, the size of the pile astounded us. This close to the finish line we felt safe continuing with very little gear.

Tyler and I emerged from our tent into the howling wind. We were raring to go. After packing up, I snapped a few hasty photos of our pile of jetsam. The wind had firmed up most of the drifts. We were even blessed with a long stretch of relatively snowless ice right out of camp. I yanked on my sled, feeling its lightness for the first time. I knew we were going to cruise.

Thirty minutes later we stopped so Tyler could tape a sore part of his foot before it turned into a blister. He'd been vigilant about this the whole trip, patiently adjusting his socks and boot liners as needed. We never hesitated to make this kind of pit stop. To allow blisters to form would be to invite misery. We looked at equipment maintenance from the same perspective. As always, it was better to fix a small problem now than grapple with an uncontrollable one later. Despite the unscheduled break, Tyler and I covered 3.5 nm in the first march, a phenomenal pace for us.

The rest of Day 52 continued in the same vein. Visibility came and went, the wind died down a little. Twelve hours on the march seemed like a vacation compared to the sixteen-hour travel days we'd been putting in. We were worn out when we hit the tent, but thrilled by our 15 nm of northward progress.

Our negative feelings evaporated with the faster pace. Knowing that we wouldn't drift much during rest periods reinforced the new vibe. Just fourteen hours earlier we couldn't have imagined feeling this pumped about our chances. I was loving the extra food, but it still wasn't enough. At this point my appetite was insatiable.

The past twenty-four hours had been emotionally draining. For the first time in days, I lay down with positive thoughts in my head, and I closed my eyes for one cherished hour of sleep. Seconds later a wheezing snort woke me up. "Tyler," I groaned, "put in your snoring device." I repeated this four times and nudged him until he stirred and grunted that he was awake.

"Your snoring device?"

"I don't have it anymore."

"What do you mean?"

"I threw it out."

Self-care to the end. Tyler stops to tape up during a march, Day 52.

Sleep boss. During the push, the beeping alarm was always minutes away.

"What?"

"I thought we agreed to throw out all nonessential items."

I was beside myself, laughing and pissed off at the same time. By the time these thoughts receded, Tyler was snoring away again, his arms dangling outside his sleeping bag. I didn't have it in me to nudge him or roll him over on his side. Sleep was more important to him than me. I was content to lie there and rest.

Forty minutes later, at 3:00 p.m. on April 23, our Victorinox alarm clock went off. We had to cover forty-one miles in the next sixty-two hours.

We took solace in a new mantra: "Safe and steady." During this twelve-hour stint the weather continued its tricks. The sun came and went, and the wind still gusted up to twenty knots.

Snow conditions had transitioned to low, rounded hummocks of shiny, sun-baked crust. This crust was so slick that the wind kept pushing our sleds sideways. We decided to try skiing without skins, the narrow nylon grips on the bottoms of our skis. After the first break we unscrewed Tyler's skins for a test, and mine soon

Another crossing complete. Tyler, Day 52.

Camp, Day 53.

after. The extra glide was remarkable.

Unfortunately, the altered balance that came with the extra glide was loading the pressure points on the bottoms of my feet in a most unwelcome way. That morning I'd finally gotten fed up with my socks. After twenty-three days of sweat and grime, they looked like they'd been dipped repeatedly in caramel sauce. The nasty cheese clung to my toes and the insides of my vapor-liner socks, which I wore between my liner socks and outer wool socks. So for the first time on the trip, I decided to wear only the wool outer socks.

Soon, hot spots began to develop on the soles of my feet, but I kept going.

Another bad choice.

Skiing with no skins through rubble was downright treacherous. Our skis now slipped where before they had gripped. Gliding across the sun-crusted hummocks, I sometimes fell as the sled jerked my body around. Tyler, who is a better skier, had no trouble staying up. But I kept crashing hard onto my butt and knees.

The crashes made me angry and zapped my energy. Meanwhile, my feet began to scream at me. When I caught up with Tyler, we agreed that skiing without skins was faster, but not worth the risk. We needed to get back on the slow-and-steady train. As Tyler reattached his skins, I put on my caramel-sauce socks and vapor

Tyler cruising, Day 54.

Weary moment. John, ninety minutes before the end of Day 54.

liners. My feet felt at home again, and I was back in control of my skis.

Tyler struggled mightily with the sleep dragon. He willed himself through the hours between 11:00 p.m. and 2:00 a.m. Later, he reported being in a dreamlike state, the kind of dream where you're running but going nowhere. I led during this stretch, which Tyler compared to Sarah taking care of Ethan in the middle of the night.

The ocean continued to challenge us. Swimming several leads and traversing sections of rubble slowed us down. We'd long since realized that we'd be dealing with rubble all the way to the Pole. Thankfully, the boost in calories helped keep our energy up. The increased food intake meant we were averaging 10,000 calories per person per day.

The second twelve-hour stint netted 12.3 nm.

I had another fleeting nap through Tyler's rasping gurgle-snorts. At least he was getting some sleep. When we awoke, Tyler was seized by a cramp in his groin. He bellowed out in pain. There wasn't much he could do about it besides stretching and being careful with his body position. We just hoped the cramps didn't get any worse over the next thirty-six hours.

We began the third twelve-hour stint at 8:00 a.m. on April 24. With a good pace we'd be able to push on to the Pole following one more nap. Our goal was to be within 15 nm by the time we put up the tent.

Misty, overcast conditions during the first two marches made everything seem soft and indistinct. I felt numb and listless, like I feel when I'm dehydrated, only hazier. Episodes of *This American Life* playing on my iPod made things even more surreal. Vivid descriptions of New York City were hard to reconcile with the world I was moving through.

On our first march we covered 3.6 nm, skiing across several newly frozen leads, one of them twice. Later on, we had to swim several more. We struggled with whiteout much of the day, but the magnetic effect of the finish line pulled us forward.

In the tent that evening we felt good. Our camp was just sixteen miles from the Pole. Tomorrow would be the last day.

After dinner I dug out the spice bottle that held the remains of our Scotch. Tyler didn't want any. I took a tiny sip and closed my eyes. I desperately wanted to get to sleep before Tyler started snoring.

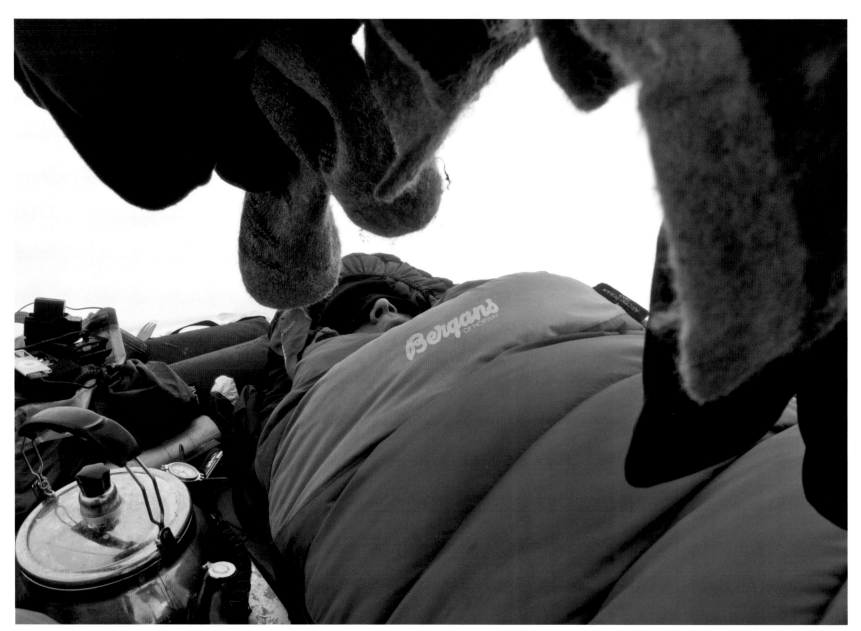

Sleep cocoon. John finally gets some Z's.

Speaking into our camera's recorder at 9:51 p.m. on April 24, we made an audio journal entry:

Tyler: There were a number of leads today. We noticed them in our noses because of the humidity.

John: The sun was in and out all day. Last night was nice and sunny—today was not. Fish, I'm going to get dinner going now. Ready. [Match strikes on box]

John: I was pretty tired on the first two marches and then felt good.

Tyler: This is my best of the three days on the new twelve-hour schedule, probably because it fits into the typical clock the most. I felt pretty good.

Tyler: Right now I'm stretching because I'm trying to avoid a cramp in my inside thigh. The terrain has been awesome.

John: We hit that lead in the right spot.

Tyler: Yeah, we did.

John: If we had hit it a little further east, we might've decided to swim it.

Tyler: [Yawning] Leads are tough because swimming is sometimes safer and faster. But if we can cross on skis, that's even better.

John: We're excited about the Pole, but very cautious with our energy. We don't know what each hour is going to be like. We might have to swim or cross a lead or go through rubble. Anything is possible. I feel we're in a good position, though.

Tyler: We trust that, given our average speed and all those things, we should have plenty of time.

John: And I think we have a friend in Victor. If we're close, he'll allow us to make it.

Tyler: I'm about to shut my eyes for a few minutes.

John: Great, I think dinner's ready pretty soon.

Although we didn't realize it till we heard the recording months later, the pace of our conversation was an exhausted crawl.

DAY 54

89° 43.856' N
040° 47.442' W

Out cold. John right before dinner, Day 54.

Nose troubles. Frostbite and snoring, Day 54, 10:35 p.m.

By John Huston   Day 55: April 25, 2009

"Whoa. That was a hard trip." —John Huston

One hour later the alarm roused me out of the netherworld of deep sleep. I felt supple and full of energy, just like you feel the first morning after getting over the flu.

Unbeknownst to me, Tyler had deliberately let me fall asleep before he went to bed. He stayed up most of the hour writing in his journal and taking photos.

The sun-bathed tent walls rippled in a gentle breeze. The break in the weather we'd been waiting for was upon us. We just hoped it would stick around.

We packed up, knowing that unless something drastic happened, we wouldn't camp again till we reached the Pole. I kept quiet, not wanting to jinx anything.

Due to the lower wind speed, we'd only drifted 0.6 nm during our three hours in the tent. That put us about 17 nm short of our goal. Navigation near the Pole can get tricky, so to reduce the variables we decided to ski directly north.

The weather held and our pace was on target. We

Last start? John sets out, Day 55, 12:20 a.m.

allowed ourselves a few extra minutes on breaks to sit behind the sleds, soaking up the sun and taking in the subtly changing panorama of multihued ice and snow—mostly white, with shades of blue and silver. Too bad we hadn't been able to enjoy more moments like this along the way.

During the past week my quadriceps tingled anytime I stood still. Today the pins and needles were worse than ever. They appeared every time I stopped to pull out the compass.

After the second break Tyler's stomach started feeling queasy. He'd mentioned this several times over the past few days, but now he was feeling weak and lightheaded, too. My stomach didn't feel right either. I wondered what was causing it.

On the previous break Tyler had given me a few nuts out of his lunch bag—known affectionately as the "Nasty Sack"—a blue zippered stuff sack he'd used since Day 1. As each new five-day ration rolled around, Tyler dumped his lunch items into the sack. Since he rarely finished his full

Nasty morsels. Tyler digs into his lunch bag, a.k.a. the Nasty Sack, an hour before leaving camp, Day 55.

Tyler takes a spill. Day 55, 5:06 a.m.

Nasty sacked. Tyler nauseated at 10:46 a.m.

Floating bridge. This perfectly placed chunk gave us the step we needed during the second march.

ration, the contents had steadily grown. It finally dawned on me that some of the food crumbs had gone rotten in the warmer tent of the past few weeks. Deep fried bacon was the likely culprit.

I hesitated to tell him. The Nasty Sack food was practically all he had.

At the next break Tyler stumbled up to me. He bent over with his hands on his knees. "I really feel like crap," he groaned. "I need to lie down." He drank a cup of pemmican soup from our Thermos, took a sip of water, and lay on his side in the snow.

"The other episodes passed after a while, but this is the worst," he mumbled. "I'll be okay in a bit. I hope."

"Try to sleep a little if you can," I said.

I mentioned that I thought it was the Nasty Sack.

"Could be," he responded. "I'll try to eat the fresher looking pieces. Or stick to truffles."

Fifteen minutes later Tyler was okay to ski again. Halfway through the next march he was feeling better.

About ten hours into our travel day we had the longest swim of the expedition. I ended up swimming first but forgot to clip the sled to the pull-loop on my foot. So I alternated between reaching behind me to break the ice with my arms, and pulling the sled along by its front handle. Eventually I left it behind me. Tyler ended

Wind-sculpted ridge. One hour into the first march.

up pulling his sled and nudging mine along with his head.

Shivering, we rolled up our drysuits. We'd been in the water fifteen minutes, by far the longest swim of the trip. After a few handfuls of lunch and some water we skied north.

I was worried that we might run into that same lead again, but it soon vanished from sight.

On the next break the GPS read 89° 54' N. Suddenly it registered in my brain that the Pole was only 6.0 nm away. We could be there in less than three marches.

It was strange to think the trip would soon be over. It would be so nice to stop skiing, to have the goal behind us, to exit our machine-like routines and, most of all, to sleep. But in some ways I didn't want it to end. In an ideal world we'd reach the Pole and relax for a day or two with an unlimited supply of guacamole and chocolate cake. We could just sit there in the tent free of stress, eating and reminiscing. But this was not to be. We barely had enough food for one final meal, and we'd likely arrive with only hours to spare before the pickup.

By this point we'd already gone beyond our twelve-hour travel day, but the thought of setting up the tent never entered our heads.

Near 89° 58' N, I stopped to check the compass against the GPS.

"I don't trust our bearing," I said. "We're too close to the Pole." At the Pole all lines of longitude intersect. If we relied solely on our compass, we could end up skiing in circles.

"I agree," Tyler said. "We should navigate with the GPS compass."

I switched to the compass screen on the DeLorme PN-40. It indicated we should be skiing 20° more to the west than our current bearing. I picked out a distant ice chunk to use as a landmark, turned off the GPS, and started skiing.

About ninety minutes later we saw a red dot on the horizon, right in our path. As we got closer, it was clear that we were skiing toward a tent. It could only be the three-man expedition guided by Lonnie Dupre. This morning Julie had said he was just a few hours ahead of us.

We skied up to Lonnie's tent. The team slept away inside. After a minute we announced ourselves. The tent unzipped and a gaunt, haggard version of Lonnie Dupre emerged, along with Stewart, one of his clients. We shook hands heartily. If Lonnie looks like that, I wondered, then what the hell do we look like?

Lonnie examined us. "Can you guys see okay? Are you hallucinating?"

Noggin nudge. Tyler pushes John's sled with his head while pulling his own with his foot.

Twelfth hour. John up front at 11:30 a.m. Route finding never gets boring.

We assured him that we were feeling pretty stable.

"You guys are really making Minnesota proud," he said. "You're about to achieve something special."

We checked the GPS. We were still one mile short of the Pole. Lonnie's camp had drifted about a mile south since he arrived there nine hours earlier.

Stewart pointed north. "It's just over that ridge. You guys are going to do it!"

"We'll see you on the helicopter tomorrow," Tyler said. We shook hands goodbye.

We should have taken a snack break while visiting Lonnie's tent, but we forgot. As we approached the ten-foot-high ridge, Tyler called for me to wait up.

Minnesotan meet-up. Tyler, John, and Lonnie Dupre about a mile from the Pole.

"We need to take a break," he groaned. "I'm not feeling well again."

"Okay. Let's rest in the lee of the ridge," I said. "What's wrong?"

"Just feeling out of it."

Five minutes later I stopped just inside an opening in the rubble at the base of the ridge. I was feeling a little impatient. We were less than half a mile from the Pole. Tyler pulled up and immediately lay down next to his pulk.

"We need to rest. I'm really feeling it. My body feels like it's ready to shut down," he said.

"Let's have some truffles and rehydrate."

"Yeah, we haven't eaten in two and a half hours. I need to put on another layer." I grabbed his water bottle, Nasty Sack, and fleece jacket from his sled and handed them over. "We're not there yet," he continued. "We're at our most tired point. We don't want to rush and do something stupid."

"Right. We don't want to be feeling low when we get there."

"Give me ten minutes to lie here. I'll be okay."

I leaned against an ice chunk while Tyler napped in the fetal position on the snow. Fifteen minutes later I woke him up and we clambered over the ridge. The

episode had passed.

On the other side I rechecked the GPS compass and picked a new landmark. Only 0.30 nm left. The North Pole was in sight. The view looked like thousands of views we had seen along the way. We knew all along that this would be the case, but it still made us smile.

The actual North Pole point was located at the bottom of the ocean, 14,000 feet below us. Of course it would be impossible to erect a marker on the ocean surface, since the ice is always drifting. That was okay. It would just be us and the ocean, the way it should be.

The final 0.30 nm went by in a blink. I checked the GPS a few times while skiing. A hundred yards from 90° N, I stopped. We were standing on the best patch of snow for staking a tent that we'd seen in two weeks. The perfect campsite right at the Pole—what could be better?

We got ready to locate the Pole itself. We removed our skis and put on our down vests. I grabbed some extra batteries. Tyler grabbed the video camera. We walked side-by-side, each of us holding a GPS. As we walked we called out the readings on the display.

"89° 59.877'." For some reason GPS devices don't read 90° N, so 89° 59.999' N was our goal.

"89° 59.920'."

"Wow. We are so close," Tyler said. The wind had come up a bit since morning. A light haze hung in the sky.

We began walking in circles, eyes riveted to our GPS screens, our fingers poised on the button that would record the coordinates of our exact location.

I called out. "I got 89° 59.995'."

For the next few minutes our paths crisscrossed one another—starting, stopping, turning, and starting again. If there'd been any onlookers, they might have thought we were performing a slow, halting, ritualistic dance.

"Here it is!" Tyler shouted. "89° 59.999'! I hit the button! We did it! We're standing at the North Pole!"

"Whoa. I can't believe it," I gasped.

We both laughed as we wearily embraced.

"Whoa," I said again. "I can't believe it. We're done."

It had only taken us twenty minutes of walking around. We were expecting two hours.

"Unbelievable!" Tyler exclaimed. "We are at the North Pole."

"Now we can sleep."

And that was it—an understated celebration. Not that we had the energy, but a raucous exultation would have seemed out of place. Instead, we turned a slow three-sixty, gazing south toward the icy horizon. It was almost as if we were thanking the ocean. We were overwhelmed by a sense of disbelief and awe.

Pole dance. Tyler homes in on the elusive northernmost point in the world.

In that moment we felt the power of the Arctic Ocean in a way that only a few people have. It was as if our bodies were acknowledging the immensity of effort required to reach this point. We felt beaten up and privileged at the same time. The ocean had brought out the best in us, and in doing so had granted us permission to succeed. It would always be the master.

The tent went up like magic. Each snow peg snugged perfectly into the surface. Once in the tent we went right into our normal routines. I lit the stove and started melting snow. Tyler began drying out his mittens.

Our supplies were down to the last remnants. We had just enough pemmican for one pot of stew. The Nasty Sack held a small collection of lunch food. One liter of fuel remained, enough for at least three days, had we needed to stretch it.

As the stoves went to work beneath the Fat Lady teapot, we got on the satellite phone and called home. First Tyler called Sarah, who was waiting for the call with Julie and a few other friends from Ely. After a short talk with Sarah, Tyler spoke

with Julie. "We were staring down the barrel of failure," he said. "Thanks for telling us not to quit."

I figured that Jennifer and my family were still on the airplane bound for Norway, so I called Kristin, our office manager. She told me they'd already landed. It was the middle of the night in Norway, but they were all up waiting for the news. Jennifer was thrilled that we made it, and relieved that it was over.

Then I called in to update the blog, thanking our sponsors and support staff.

We toasted with our last nip of Scotch. "I'm proud of us," Tyler said.

"Me, too," I said. "We really took care of each other."

We woke up three hours later. "Time to get up, Fish."

Tyler groaned. Concrete had been poured into our blood vessels as we slept.

"Ohh, my legs. Holy crikey," I moaned. "Total muscle rigor mortis!"

"Oh, man. I've never felt like this," Tyler said.

Our bodies were pinned to the floor. We literally had to command ourselves to move each individual limb.

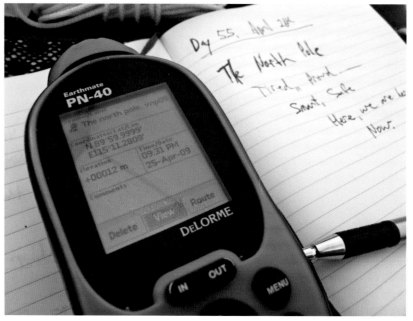

Final entry. We reached the pole at 5:31 p.m. CST. The GPS is set to a different time zone.

Victory pose. The last camp.

Empty of energy.

"Either the extra sleep let our muscles stiffen up, or our minds have flipped the switch that shows up at the finish line."

"I bet it's some of both. Whatever it is, it's powerful."

Helicopter noises thumped in the background.

Civilization, in the form of a hulking orange-and-blue Russian helicopter, landed a hundred yards away. Victor and a few passengers ran over. We snapped photos and hurriedly packed our sleds. We stepped into the helicopter belly to a hearty greeting from Lonnie's team and Keith and Sebastian, who'd been picked up just north of 89° N.

It felt like the body panels were going to rattle loose as the aged beast lifted off the ice. It was hard to talk above the whapping rotors. Below, the ridges and pans of ice looked small and distant.

In early April, the Barneo base had been installed a few miles from the North Pole. Since then it had drifted to 88° N. In the next hour we flew a distance that had taken us almost two weeks to ski.

We were back in the company of others, but I was numb to it. Tyler talked with the other passengers. I closed my eyes and tried to sleep.

Big bird. The Russian MI-8 approaches.

Walk of the weary.

In the tent that night we flipped on the audio recorder. Here are some excerpts:

Tyler: Holy cow! John and I are sitting at the North Pole in our tent. We have officially succeeded.

Tyler: We are tired.
John: The energy at the moment is with us. I think we were more tired on some marches than we are right now. There were some hard moments today.

John: Want to split a truffle to start?
Tyler: Yeah, happily.
John: I cannot tell you how much I appreciate your donations.
Tyler: Where's my Nasty Sack?

John: I'll start cooking dinner.
John: Okay, dinner, dinner, dinner.
John: So you want to eat dinner and then take a nap, or should we celebrate more? I think we should celebrate some more.
Tyler: I think we should celebrate some more. It's a good time for that.
John: Is all the butter already in there? Whoa, what a good butter slick.
Tyler: Yeah.

John: Wow, it was hard. But I never wanted to tell myself how hard it actually was. But it is just a frickin' beat down, tirelessly! You can never let your guard down.
Tyler: Just when you think you can predict it, you can't.

John: My tongue is so burnt. All this food I've been looking forward to, it's going to hurt me.
Tyler: Crispy bacon, hmm, so good.

John: We had no joint problems. Can you believe that?! That is un-be-lieve-able!
Tyler: Do you know how much pain medication we took?
John: None.
Tyler: Not even ibuprofen.
John: I just took some Excedrin for a few headaches.

John: We were smart tough the whole way.
Tyler: We were smart tough? Yeah, we were.

Tyler: How much sleep will we get tonight?
John: Three hours.
Tyler: That's a lot.
John: Okay, let's do it, let's go to sleep!
John: We did it, bro! Unbelievable trip!
Tyler: In the beginning the weather was so nice. So many days of sun.
John: It was crazy cold though. Okay, Fish, ready for bed?
Tyler: Yep.

Glowing. And going home.

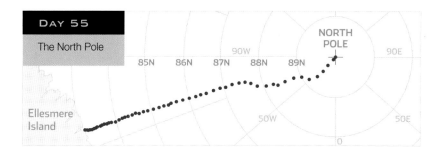

DAY 55
The North Pole

13 APRÈS-SKI

BY JOHN HUSTON

"Now we learn you party." —Recent Norwegian proverb

When the helicopter landed at Barneo, it was 0° F and windy. Tyler and I stood around with the other expeditioners and adventure tourists waiting for the flight to Svalbard, Norway. I couldn't stay warm while standing still, so I boarded the jet as soon as I could and took a nap.

Twenty minutes later, Tyler and everyone else filed onto the plane. Victor passed out glasses of Russian brandy. We soon dozed off and slept for most of the two-and-a-half-hour flight.

We landed in Svalbard in the late afternoon of April 26. Still dressed in our smelly expedition clothes, we caught a ride to the supermarket. I scarfed down three Snickers ice cream bars right there in the freezer aisle. Tyler ate two bananas. We stocked up on chocolate, potato chips, and bread. I bought a razor and a squeeze tube of bacon flavored cheese. Then we were off to the hotel.

One down, one to go. In flight to Svalbard.

Courtesy of Lonnie Dupre

Antonov An-74. Barneo base camp, Day 56, 5:40 a.m.

The first shower was a shock. My butt had been reduced to a flap of skin. My armpits were like caves. I was touching a body that wasn't mine.

Tyler and I walked to a nearby pub for our first meal. Since our arrival we'd been downing the chocolates and Reese's Peanut Butter Cups my mother had sent to the hotel. This was fun—our metabolisms still thought we were on expedition.

The pub bustled with adventure tourists. We didn't see any open tables, so I asked the bartender for help, explaining that my friend and I had just completed a long and difficult trip. Her response caught me off guard: "Everyone here says they've been on a big trip."

Huh. "Welcome to Norway," I thought.

Half an hour later, following a phone interview with the *Chicago Sun-Times*, Tyler and I sat at a table with beers and a plate of fries. We toasted our health and success and dug in. After one bite we stopped. We looked at each other sadly. "I don't taste anything," I said.

"Me either."

"Ugh. We burned our taste buds with all the hot stew."

"Well, at least chocolate tastes good." We finished our main meal and ordered two desserts each.

At 2:00 a.m. we boarded a plane for the mainland. We buzzed with a wacky energy fueled by sleep deprivation, the twenty-four-hour sunlight, and our return to civilization. We'd only slept a few hours since reaching the Pole twenty-six hours earlier.

On the plane Tyler and I struggled mightily to peel back the foil from our orange juice cups, but we just couldn't do it. Our fingertips were numb. After dragging our sleds through a changeover at Tromsø Airport, we began the final leg of the flight. The jolt of the plane hitting the runway woke me up. I glimpsed airport

Body shock. Tyler in Svalbard. First bathroom, first shower, first look at a new person.

Courtesy of Harald Kippenes

Huston hurray. John's family and Jennifer at the Oslo airport. The big cake awaits.

Courtesy of Harald Kippenes

First hug. John and Jennifer.

buildings speeding by and went right back to sleep. Two minutes later, I woke up again and asked Tyler when we were going to land. He chuckled and told me we were on the ground in Oslo.

It was Monday, April 27, around 7:30 a.m., and the airport was nearly empty. All I could think about was finding Jennifer and my family. I spotted them on the other side of the security gate, holding a homemade welcome banner and waving American flags. They looked so quaint to me, standing huddled next to a small table that held a giant chocolate sheet cake and several bottles of champagne. Jennifer was there, along with my mom and dad, my sister and her husband, my brother, and Harald

How much can I eat?

This much, says Tyler.

Father and son. Tyler and Ethan, together for the first time in eleven weeks. Oslo, April 27.

Kippenes, my good friend and Greenland expedition teammate. Their beaming faces lit up the terminal.

I embraced Jennifer first. She was crying and looked worn out. After big hugs from everyone else, Tyler and I spent the next thirty minutes devouring the cake and downing glasses of champagne. It seemed like my mother cried the entire time. Then, we all headed to Harald's flat for a huge brunch of eggs, hash browns, and about a gallon of guacamole.

Later that day Tyler and I drove back to the airport with Harald to meet Sarah, Ethan, and Sarah's father, who had come in on a later flight. Somehow we missed them. The grand moment they'd all been hoping for was gone. Tyler was bummed. When they finally met up a few hours later at the hotel, Tyler saw Ethan's

Tyler and Rune.

blonde hair and two front teeth for the first time. But it was time for Ethan's nap and the atmosphere was subdued. While Ethan napped, Sarah and Tyler talked quietly. They were glad to see each other, but they were both worn out, and their disappointment from the flubbed reunion would take a while to get over.

We spent the next few days in Oslo, eating, fielding interview requests from the States, and trying to relax with our families. Weeks of daydreaming on the ice had

heightened our expectations beyond reality. Tyler and I rarely saw each other, which didn't feel right. We were both experiencing an emotional cocktail of adrenaline, deep exhaustion, and the desire to be good hosts to our families. It was all a blur.

Back on the twenty-four-hour clock, we yearned for more hours in the day. Powerfully vivid dreams dominated our sleep. The moment we closed our eyes, we relived scenes from the push to the Pole and all the stress that went with it. At times we woke up screaming from leg cramps. My thighs wouldn't stop tingling.

Polar Mecca. The Fram Museum. The famous ship rests indoors.

Tyler, Sarah, and Ethan. Arriving at the Fram celebration.

Fram Museum celebration. Oslofjord, Norway.

The frostbitten tip of Tyler's nose turned into a dime-sized scab that simply fell off, leaving no trace. After a few days our taste buds began to recover, but our dreams of bursting flavors were not meant to be realized in Oslo.

The April 29 celebration at the Fram Museum on the Oslofjord was one of the greatest nights of our lives. The Fram Museum houses the *Fram*, the ship Amundsen sailed to Antarctica in 1911. (*Fram*, which translates as "forward" in English, was the inspiration for the name of our expedition company, Forward Expeditions.) We joined Rune, Harald, several directors from Bergans of Norway, our families, and the rest of our Norwegian friends on the deck of the *Fram* itself. There, we presented the highlights of our trip, followed by drinks and a sumptuous buffet. To celebrate on our hero's ship while surrounded by the most important people in our lives was truly extraordinary. Afterward, forty of us took over the Fritjof Nansen pub, where we partied until it closed at 3:00 a.m. Tyler and I couldn't keep up with all the drinks put in front of us, or the increasingly raucous energy of people letting loose on our behalf.

EPILOGUE

BY JOHN HUSTON

"On arrival, the journey begins." —Marcel Mariën

After the party in Oslo my life felt like a blank screen. The expedition had so consumed me that I couldn't picture my life after it. When I tried to, all I saw was black.

I spent the summer of 2009 relaxing with Jennifer, eating way too much, and working with our sponsors, but during that time I felt numb and detached. Tyler and I knew all along that we wanted to write a book, but it wasn't until much later that my mind cleared up enough to start writing.

Now it all seems so far away. My life at home is so different from life on the ice. I do a lot of sitting. I sit staring at my computer. I sit in my car, which sits in traffic. I sit in an airport terminal waiting to go sit on a plane. I miss the immediacy of expedition life, the sheer physicality and exposure to the elements. My mind and body are numbed by the comforts of modern civilization. At the same time I appreciate sleeping in a bed, eating fresh fruit, and talking to people other than my tent-mate.

I split my time between commercial real estate and expedition work. During the springs of 2010 and 2011, I was a guide at the scientific camp where Tyler was based in 2010. About once a month I give motivational talks to corporate and student audiences. I also run logistics and safety for other polar expeditions. New opportunities in the expedition world are always popping up. I'm not quite ready for another big project, but I'm getting there.

My premonition about Jennifer turned out to be true. On August 27, 2011, we were married on a bluff overlooking Lake Michigan. In some ways planning the wedding felt like planning an expedition—the ultimate expedition will be marriage itself.

Tyler and I talk at least once a week. We talk about the book, other expeditions we've worked on, our time on the ice, and life in general, and we laugh a lot more than we did in the past. I appreciate his quiet steadfastness, his generosity, and his grounded character. Writing this book has been like a yearlong version of one of those slow, meandering, multi-march conversations we had on the ice—a wonderfully dispassionate discussion of our perspectives, memories, and time together. It has provided closure to the experience and deepened our brother-like bond.

I still think about our North Pole journey every day. Sometimes I ponder the ways in which it has impacted my life. Other times I just recall a scene from the ice. It's impossible to imagine who I would be if I hadn't taken on the challenge. Sure, I can picture myself in a different daily life, but the experience is forever ingrained in my character. That's what I can't imagine being different.

People always want to know what I learned on the way to the Pole. Often I shy away from the question. It's too much like the "Why?" question. Still, I can offer some answers by simply considering what I'd do differently next time.

Make the team dynamic a top priority: Tyler and I needed more structured opportunities to build a healthier relationship. Regular check-ins and assistance from a third party would have alleviated much of the below-the-surface tension.

Get off the grid: If it were up to me, I wouldn't send blogs or upload photos. Dealing with all the electronics was a huge pain and made me feel like I was right back at the office. That took away from the moment. I yearn for the total immersion of the explorer of yesteryear. In today's world it's becoming increasingly difficult to disconnect. The result is a disconnection of the mind and body. My mind spent a lot of time in the office when my body was on the Arctic Ocean.

Don't do it all yourself: I wanted the whole enchilada, the full-on, down-and-dirty expedition journey. I got it and then some. Once was enough. I'm still not recovered from the sheer massif of effort this project siphoned out of me. I'll know I'm recovered when I feel ready for another big trip. Next time I'll delegate a whole lot more, plan even further ahead, and try to keep my schedule sane. To do otherwise would be to risk burnout and miss all the fun. I can still feel the crush of those sleepless nights in Resolute.

Remember the ones at home—it's harder on them: Expeditions are inherently selfish. The really hard ones require a singleness of focus. When we're on the ice we are super engaged in our own little world. Since we're pushing our limits, we can be mentally fragile. That means we're not able to fully support our loved ones. Instead, we ask them to nurture and baby us so as not to upset our dialed-in mental state. This can be too much to ask of the people we leave behind, considering the worry, loneliness, and isolation they may experience. I'm lucky Jennifer is such an independent person. Next time, though, I'll be more deliberate about trying to minimize the impact on her.

I'm happy that the biggest lesson from the expedition didn't come from what went wrong. It came from what went right. After all, our grand plan worked!

Learning takes time, and a lot of patience. We had never been on the Arctic Ocean, never run a fundraising campaign, and never done a two-month unsupported expedition. We had a solid foundation of skills, but we knew it would take a few years to build on that. Looking at our goal from a long-term perspective was a major key to our success.

Our stated values—optimism, humility, and responsibility—brought Tyler and me together as a team. They kept us together all the way to the Pole and beyond. It's fair to say that without a strong commitment to these values, our relationship would have crumbled. The values gave us direction. They anchored our integrity and allowed us to create lasting relationships with our mentors, our sponsors, and our charity partner—CaringBridge.org.

Since our inspiration came from the historic and modern explorers who had gone before, we wanted our project to honor them. Not to do so would have been disrespectful. As it turned out, synthesizing the methods of our heroes gave us a blueprint for success. Asking ourselves how Amundsen would prepare for an endeavor, or what Rune would do to overcome an obstacle, helped us set high standards and encouraged us to do things the right way.

Five years ago we took the risk. We had a big dream and we went after it hard. We knew the journey would be arduous, that it would push us to new levels, that we'd be challenged to adapt, that success would be earned through sweat and persistence. But that's exactly what we wanted.

EPILOGUE

BY TYLER FISH

"The highest reward for a man's toil is not what he gets for it, but what he becomes by it." —John Ruskin

It's April 4, 2011. I'm writing this while flying over the sea ice in a DC-3, heading toward the North Pole. I've been hired to co-lead a ski expedition from the Pole to Greenland.*

With every pressure ridge and lead I see below, I'm reminded of something from 2009 that I don't want to forget but no doubt will. Most memories just don't last. That's probably one reason for writing this book—and why I'm heading back.

Life on the ice is simple. Maybe that means my everyday mind is just too complicated. Expeditions are a relief from that.

The immediacy and focus of the lifestyle can result in deep friendships forged in a matter of weeks. My ex-teammates understand me better than some friends I've known for years.

John and I have a closer bond now than when we left Ward Hunt in search of the Pole. I'm really proud of that. I respect him greatly for dedicating his energy, his critical mind, and three years of his life to our success. I understand him so well—his moods and words, his own unique wisdom, and (usually) his sense of humor.

He and I are the only ones who really know what happened during those fifty-five days. We're bonded in a way that's impossible to share with anyone else. The whole experience is hard to explain, and at times that's disappointing. But for anyone who has faced such a challenge, it doesn't need explaining.

Last year while working as a guide 270 nm northwest of Resolute, I was given some sage advice by my colleague, Paul Ramsden. Paul, who has completed well over a hundred first ascents on mountains and rock walls all over the world, had this to say about our North Pole trip: "You can never do that again. It will never be the same. That was a first for you and a first. You could do the exact same trip again and it would never feel the same. It's impossible."

I responded with a quote from *The Life of Pi*, by Yann Martel: "First wonder goes deepest; wonder after that fits in the impression made by the first." We didn't need to say more.

---

*Due to heavy weather, the flight never reached the North Pole—the farthest north we got was 88° 19.67' N. We started skiing south from there. Time constraints, priorities of scientific research, and the filming of a documentary turned the trip into a journey from "nowhere to nowhere," but still worth it.

I also took Paul's words as a warning. I had assumed I would eventually long for a repeat of 2009. But now I realized that could never happen.

There are some aspects of my next trip that I don't want to be the same. I'll see to it that I don't put my family through the stress of 2009. Readjusting to Outward Bound, my home on Wilson Street in Ely, and my wife and son was the hardest thing I've ever done, I think. It took six months to recover some sort of balance to life.

I was physically fine, apart from feet that ached every morning and an appetite that wouldn't quit. In Oslo I'd asked Rune, "How long will I be hungry?" He told me that in two weeks I'd be fat. He was right. Two weeks later I was right back at my pre-expedition weight, and not happy about it.

For several years before the expedition my life had been so heavy and busy, cluttered and over-programmed. Relationships had borne the brunt of it. Now I needed to relearn how to be a coworker and a husband. Fatherhood . . . I basically had to start over.

I wasn't ready for life after the North Pole. On the ocean I had accepted everything in stride. At home that wasn't so easy. I returned full of big ideas for making changes in my life, but I had no idea how to execute them. I felt like a stranger in a strange land, a place that should've felt familiar but didn't. When old patterns reemerged, I was devastated. Countless distracting details crowded in.

"Do less, and do it better," I told myself. My new philosophy was born of memories of simplicity and strength on the ice.

Since that time of struggle, I've come to terms with my optimism. Belief alone doesn't get you what you want. Faith in your abilities is not enough. You have to adapt. You have to do things differently without giving up the core of who you are. John and I did this and succeeded. So has my family.

My relationship with Sarah and Ethan is stronger than ever. The decision for me to return to the Arctic Ocean was a joint one. Getting out the door was still hectic, but I refused to sacrifice time with my family. We've communicated a lot more since I left home and I've tried to be more mindful of their situation.

I look out the frosty window to the ice below. In a few hours I'll be down there in the rubble, hauling my heavy pulk, immersed in the familiar routines. I wonder how much I'll be thinking of 2009, and how this trip will change my view of that one.

In the end an expedition is like a piece of art. You plan it, you do it, you succeed or fail. Then you give it up for review. You may not like what people remember, because it doesn't represent the whole of the thing, or even the best parts, or the truth for that matter. People will remember that John went through the ice, that I vented for a good while on Day 47, that we ate a lot of bacon and butter and chocolate and didn't sleep at the end, and that, yes, we made it.

We'll never be the same. We can't go back. Wouldn't want to.

We can only go forward, better.

Date	Day	Start N Lattitude	Start W Longitude	Camp N Lattitute	Camp W Longitude	Hours	NM	°F AM	°F PM	Overnight Drift NM	Wind (knots)	Notes
3/2/09	1			83 08.096	074 05.863	2:20	1.7		-35		Calm, then slight breeze	Drop off at Ward Hunt Island.
3/3/09	2			83 08.900	074 04.000	5:30	0.9	-42	-30		Calm, then slight breeze E	First lead. Ward Hunt Ice Shelf.
3/4/09	3			83 10.321	074 02.347	6:00	1.4	-47	-42		Calm	Rubble!
3/5/09	4			83 12.930	074 04.659	7:00	2.6	-56	-60		Calm	Rubble!
3/6/09	5			83 14.665	074 03.906	7:20	1.9	-56	-58		Calm	Rubble!
3/7/09	6			83 15.629	074 03.711	7:45	1.0	-56	-52		Calm	Rubble!
3/8/09	7			83 19.526	074 02.124	6:50	3.9	-38	-38		Calm, EEN 5	Low visibility. Poor contrast.
3/9/09	8			83 23.071	074 05.560	8:00	3.6	-34	-34		Calm, then breeze	
3/10/09	9			83 26.481	074 07.548	8:00	3.4	-34	-36		WNW 5	
3/11/09	10			83 31.120	074 12.118	8:20	4.7	-36	-22		ENE 5-10	
3/12/09	11			83 34.624	074 16.444	8:15	3.6	-34	-34		ENE 5-10	
3/13/09	12			83 39.218	074 18.230	8:50	4.6	-38	-34		ENE 5-10	
3/14/09	13			83 42.945	074 16.712	8:30	3.7	-42	-34		N -> SW in PM 5-10	Rubble. Snow waves. Two well-frozen leads.
3/15/09	14			83 46.166	074 18.091	8:30	3.2	-36	-26	-	W 10	Overcast. Two leads. Colossus. Old ice.
3/16/09	15			83 50.895	074 13.889	8:30	4.8	-34	-24	-	SW	Heavy snow waves. Old ice. One lead.
3/17/09	16			83 56.895	074 10.629	8:30	6.0	-36	-39		WSW	Low contrast. Heavy snow waves. One lead.
3/18/09	17			84 03.749	074 12.166	9:00	6.9	-39	-26		N	Good visibility turned to low contrast. Three leads.
3/19/09	18			84 09.479	074 21.600	9:00	5.8	-24	-24		Breeze E	Clear skies. Old ice. Rubble.
3/20/09	19			84 14.690	074 34.734	9:00	5.4	-36	-32		Calm	Clear skies then overcast to clear. Old ice. Newly crumpled leads.
3/21/09	20			84 19.798	074 43.714	9:30	5.2	-36	-22		Breeze NE	Sun in and out. Old ice with a few leads.
3/22/09	21			84 26.566	074 40.362	9:30	6.8	-16	-12		Breeze NE	New ice with ridges.
3/23/09	22			84 32.676	074 40.639	9:00	6.1	-22	-22		SW 10-15	Mostly overcast. Visibility okay.
3/24/09	23			84 39.113	074 35.186	8:10	6.5	-34	-24	0.4 N	SW 10-15	Mostly overcast. Visibility okay.
3/25/09	24			84 46.801	074 28.952	9:30	7.3	-30	-28		Calm, SSW puffs	Clear, sunny.
3/26/09	25			84 54.501	074 30.444	9:30	7.9	-40	-28	0.2 N	NNE puffs, calm	Clear, sunny. Flat ice with some waves, 1.5-mile frozen lead.
3/27/09	26			85 03.187	074 37.884	9:40	8.7	-42	-30		NNE 1-3	Clear, sunny. Flat ice with two big frozen leads, mostly good going.
3/28/09	27			85 12.012	074 30.104	9:30	8.9	-39	-28		NNE in AM, W in PM 1-2	Clear, sunny.
3/29/09	28			85 19.943	074 39.113	9:30	8.0	-38	-28		Calm	Sunny all day. New ice. Last march huge ice rubble.
3/30/09	29			85 27.343	074 34.404	9:30	7.4	-32	-28	0.3 ENE	Calm, windy later in day	Overcast with wind late in the day.
3/31/09	30			85.31.933	074 46.189	10:00	5.0	-32	-30	1.0 E	AM SW 10-12, PM SW 5-8	

Date	Day	Start N Lattitude	Start W Longitude	Camp N Lattitute	Camp W Longitude	Hours	NM	°F AM	°F PM	Overnight Drift NM	Wind (knots)	Notes
4/1/09	31			85 40.465	074 43.522	10:00	8.8	-36	-26	0.3 ESE	SW 4	Clear, sunny.
4/2/09	32			85 49.898	074 42.598	10:00	9.4	-30	-24		SW 2-4	Mix, good going, 3 leads, warm in the sun.
4/3/09	33			86 00.274	074 46.742	10:30	10.4	-22	-20		Calm, SW puffs	Mix of ice, some old, mostly flat.
4/4/09	34			86 11.503	074 50.097	10:00	11.2	-20	-20		Calm, NE puffs	Mostly new ice, last two marches older ice.
4/5/09	35	86 11.667	074 49.368	86 20.510	074 53.601	8:00	8.8	-22	-18	0.2 NNE	Calm, SE puffs	Mostly newer ice, last march lead N.
4/6/09	36			86 30.177	074 57.139	10:00	9.7	-22	-20	0.1 NNE	Calm, SE puffs	One newly frozen one-mile lead, mix of ice, new, old, heavy.
4/7/09	37	86 30.494	074 55.590	86 41.674	075 00.830	10:00	11.2	-26	-20	0.3 NNE	Calm SSE puffs	
4/8/09	38	86 42.095	074 58.603	86 53.747	075 11.969	10:00	11.7	-30	-24	0.4 NNE	SSE 2-4	Clear. One lead 150 m across. Good going.
4/9/09	39	86 53.708	075 13.381	87 03.322	075 12.951	10:00	9.7	-22	-18	0.1 SE	NNE 4-8	Clear. Old Ice, 6 leads. Heavy all day!
4/10/09	40	87 02.951	075 18.588	87 13.047	075 19.632	11:00	10.1	-18	-17	0.4 SSW	E 4-8	Clear and a bit hazy. Big messes of ice.
4/11/09	41	87 12.725	075 17.797	87 24.302	075 27.120	11:00	11.6	-20	-20	0.4 SSE	NE -> NNW	Clear, high clouds, new ice.
4/12/09	42	87 23.546	075 11.245	87 34.015	074 52.656	11:00	10.5	-18	-18	1.0 SSE	NW -> WSW 10-14	Overcast, Changing, Good visibility.
4/13/09	43	87 33.501	074 06.805	87 41.772	073 33.662	10:30	8.4	-20	-16	2.0 E	W-WSW 10-15	Clear. Hard pack snow.
4/14/09	44	87 40.412	072 27.130	87 50.579	070 42.310	11:30	11.0	-16	-10	2.0 ESE	W-WSW 10-15	Clear. Hard pack snow.
4/15/09	45	87 49.150	069 10.429	88 03.593	068 27.494	13:00	14.5	-10	-8	3.8 SE	W-WSW 10-15	Overcast PM.
4/16/09	46	88 02.780	067 12.103	88 15.531	066 53.278	13:00	12.3	-8	-10	2.3 ESE	W-WSW 4-10	Calmer in evening. Hard pack snow.
4/17/09	47	88 14.460	065 48.568	88 22.600	064 47.195	13:00	8.2	?	?	3.0 ESE	W-WNW 7-15	
4/18/09	48	88 20.615	063 46.073	88 33.778	065 03.242	13:00	13.3	-8	-6	0.5-1.0 ESE	W-WNW 5	
4/19/09	49	88 33.350	062 54.118	88 48.391	063 32.578	15:30	15.1	-6	-2	3.3 SSE	SW 15-20, NW 4-8	White out. Low visibility AM and early PM. Started rolling the clock.
4/20/09	50	88 45.478	057 57.451	89 00.325	059 30.651	15:30	15.0	-6	-10	7.7 SE	NW-SW 10-15	Low contrast, clearing in second half of the day.
4/21/09	51	88 56.709	055 46.682	89 08.131	051 20.827	16:00	12.3	-2	0	5.4 SSE	W 10-25	Variable visibility, contrast changing every 3-4 hours.
4/22/09	52	89 05.496	046 47.746	89 20.353	044 13.876	12:30	15.0	?	?	5.0 SE	W-WNW 20-25	Variable visibility, contrast changing every 3-4 hours.
4/23/09	53	89 19.632	042 50.714	89 31.944	042 17.048	12:00	12.3	?	?	1.2 SE	W-WNW 15-20	Variable visibility, contrast changing every 3-4 hours.
4/24/09	54	89 31.225	041 19.400	89 43.856	040 47.442	12:30	12.7	?	?	0.9 SE	W-WNW 10-15	Low contrast for first 5 hours, then clearing.
4/25/09	55	89 43.393	039 26.170	89 59.999		16:40	17.6	?	?	0.6 SSE	W-NW 5	Hazy, but good contrast most of the day.

CAMPING EQUIPMENT

	Weight of item (grams)	Number of item	Total weight (grams)
Bergans of Norway Arctic Ocean Sleeping Bag	2,100	2	4,200
Bergans of Norway Extreme Sleeping Mat	618	4	2,472
Bergans of Norway Seat Mat Waffle Floor Pad	50	3	150
Crazy Creek Hexalite Long Back Camp Chair	510	2	1,020
Custom Sleeping Bag	1,105	4	4,420
Granite Gear Zipp Sack	123	8	984
Integral Designs Silcoat Stuff Sack	25	8	200
Integral Designs Sleeping Bag Vapor Liner Long	178	4	712
Lifelink Snow Shovel	810	1	810
MEC Snow Pegs with 10cm rope leash	44	6	264
Moleskine Journal	332	2	664
Pack Towels	6	2	12
Pee Bottle Square Nalgene 1L	110	2	220
Petzl Myo RXP Headlamp	100	2	200
Plumber Candle	50	1	50
Space Pen	26	2	52
Tent Brush	152	1	152
Thermarest Trail Short Sleeping Pad	544	2	1088
Thermometer	62	1	62
Toilet Paper Roll	186	10	1,860
Weber Arctic Tent Custom	2,075	1	2,075
Subtotal (kilograms)			**21.7**

COOKING EQUIPMENT

	Weight of item (grams)	Number of item	Total weight (grams)
Brunton Wind Screen Thick	80	1	80
Cardboard Fuel Box	705	3	2,115
Fat Lady Teapot with MSR Heat Exchanger	962	1	962
Fuel cans, 1 gallon	400	11	4,400
Fuel Funnels with/ Screen, Small	38	2	76
GSI Fairshare 1 Liter Bowl	210	2	420
GSI Cascadian Cup	70	2	140
Light My Fire Plastic Spoon Fork	16	3	48
Liters of Fuel	700	45.4	31,780
Matchboxes	78	2	156
Metal Stove Board Large	380	1	380
Metal Stove Board Medium	226	1	226
Metal Stove Board Small	150	1	150
MSR Alpine Spoon	28	1	28
MSR BlackLite 3L Pot with MSR Heat Exchanger	438	1	438
MSR BlackLite Pot Top	166	1	166
MSR Fuel 1.5L Bottle	220	4	880
MSR Panhandler	44	1	44
MSR Whisperlite Extra Pump	66	2	132
MSR Whisperlite International Stove	342	4	1,368
Nalgene Bottle	190	8	1,520
Granite Gear Aquatherm	130	8	1,040
Thermos Vacuum 61oz Insulated Beverage Bottle	1,186	1	1,186
Wooden Spoon	22	1	22
Subtotal (kilograms)			**47.8**

FIREARM AND ACCESSORIES

	Weight of item (grams)	Number of item	Total weight (grams)
Bergans of Norway Shotgun Case Custom	400	1	400
Bird Shot Shotgun Shells	48	10	480
Cracker Shotgun Shells	18	10	180
Winchester 12-gauge Shotgun Model 1300 NRA Coastal Marine Defender	2,948	1	2,948
Slugs	44	10	440
Subtotal (kilograms)			**4.4**

FOOTWEAR

	Weight of item (grams)	Number of item	Total weight (grams)
America's Alpaca Heavyweight Wool Socks (Pair)	158	3	474
Icebreaker Ski Mid Over-the-Calf Socks (Pair)	100	2	200
Icebreaker Ski Liner Over-the-Calf Socks (Pair)	51	3	153

	Weight of item (grams)	Number of item	Total weight (grams)
2XU Compression Liner Socks (Pair)	50	3	150
MEC Synthetic Camp Booties (Pair)	308	2	616
Intergral Designs VB Vapor Liner Socks (Pair)	80	3	240
Gator Neoprene Liner Socks (Pair)	100	2	200
Alfa Mørdre Extreme Ski Boot with Wool Liner and Custom Insulated Gaitor (Pair)	3,500	2	7,000
Sole Signature EV Ultra Insoles (Pair)	147	2	294
Subtotal (kilograms)			**9.3**

FOOD

	Weight of item (grams)	Number of item	Total weight (grams)
Food			116,000
Spices/Vitamins	1,550	1	1,550
Subtotal (kilograms)			**117.6**

HANDWEAR

	Weight of item (grams)	Number of item	Total weight (grams)
Bergans of Norway Down Mittens (Pair)	246	1	246
Brynje Liner Mittens (Pair)	30	6	180
Shell Mittens (Pair)	332	2	664
Wintergreen Fleece Mittens (Pair)	226	2	452
Subtotal (kilograms)			**1.5**

HEADWEAR

	Weight of item (grams)	Number of item	Total weight (grams)
Bergans of Norway Headband	30	2	60
Brynje Arctic Double Balaclava	86	2	172
Brynje Arctic Double Hat	60	1	60
Bergans of Norway Birkebeiner Hat	60	1	60
Gator Masks	36	4	144
Oakley Crowbar Goggles with Custom Wind Blocker	164	3	492
Wintergreen Neck Gator	48	2	96
Oakley Radar Sunglasses	40	4	160
Wapati Woolie Hat	178	2	356
Subtotal (kilograms)			**1.6**

CLOTHING LAYERS

	Weight of item (grams)	Number of item	Total weight (grams)
Bergans of Norway Antarctic Bibs	838	2	1,676
Bergans of Norway Down Vest	594	2	1,188
Bergans of Norway Antarctic Jacket with/ Ruff	767	2	1,534
Helly Hansen Drysuit Custom	1,700	2	3,400
Bergans of Norway Ulstein Fleece	572	2	1,144
Bergans of Norway Sula Fleece	604	2	1,208
Brynje Super Thermo Polo Shirt	197	4	788
Brynje Super Thermo Zip Polo Shirt	197	2	394
Brynje Double Arctic Zip Polo	597	2	1,194
Saxx Performance Boxer Brief	142	4	568
Brynje Super Thermo Longs Legs	138	3	414
Brynje Super Thermo Boxer Shorts with Wind Cover	86	2	172
Brynje Double Arctic Longs Legs with Fly	322	2	644
Wintergreen Fleece Bibs (Short and Modified)	428	2	856
Icebreaker Bodyfit 200 Legging with Fly	170	1	170
Subtotal (kilograms)			**15.4**

MEDICAL SUPPLIES

	Weight of item (grams)	Number of item	Total weight (grams)
Adventure Medical Kit Ultrlight/Watertight Pro	2,300	1	2,300
Baby Wipes	2	20	40
Soap	12	1	12
Dermatone Facial Sunblock Stick	48	2	96
Dermatone Lip Balm	16	2	32
Dermatone Skin Protection Crème with Zinc Oxide	38	6	228
Subtotal (kilograms)			**2.7**

MISCELLANEOUS

	Weight of item (grams)	Number of item	Total weight (grams)
Flags, Banners	230	1	230
Journals, Letters, Personal Items	1,000	1	1,000
Subtotal (kilograms)			**0.2**

	Weight of item (grams)	Number of item	Total weight (grams)
NAVIGATION EQUIPMENT			
Brunton Compass 15TDCLQ	85	1	85
Brunton 15TDCLQ Compass on Belt	295	1	295
DeLorme PN-40 GPS	204	2	408
Victorinox Alarm Clock	82	1	82
Subtotal (kilograms)			**0.9**
REPAIR TOOLS AND SUPPLIES			
Repair Kit	1,786	1	1,786
Victorinox Swiss Army Soldiers Knife	128	1	128
Victorinox SwissTool Spirit Plus Ratchet	208	2	416
Subtotal (kilograms)			**2.3**
SKI EQUIPMENT			
Acapulka Pulks (Set of 2, 160 cm and 130 cm)	18,100	2	36,200
Braided 6 mm Polyrope	630	1	630
Throw Bag Custom	192	2	384
Dog Sled Bungee	102	2	204
GV Aerolight 8x25 inch Snowshoes	2,200	2	4,400
Bergans of Norway Helium Backpack Custom	1,400	2	2,800
Petzl Spirit Carabiner	46	8	368
Rope 8 mm	316	1	316
Swix Ski Poles Custom	250	6	1,500
Åsnes Amundsen Skis with			
Rotefella Supertelemark Bindings (Pair)	2,370	2	4,740
Subtotal (kilograms)			**51.5**

	Weight of item (grams)	Number of item	Total weight (grams)
CAMERA AND COMMUNICATIONS EQUIPMENT			
8AA Battery Charger Custom with Batteries	226	3	678
AA Energizer Lithium Batteries	14	200	2,800
AAA Energizer Lithium Batteries	4	10	40
Camera Stand	62	1	62
Canon G10 Camera Accessories	406	1	406
Canon G10 Camera	400	2	800
Go Pro Video Camera	210	1	210
Pelican Case	538	2	1,076
HP iPaq	202	1	202
HP iPaq Accessories	30	1	30
Apple iPods and Accessories	346	1	346
Iridium Phone 9505A	368	2	736
Iridium Extras	528	1	528
Iridium Satellite Phone Battery	72	2	144
Video Camera Accessories	600	1	600
Sony HDR-CX12 Video Camera	544	1	544
Olympus u790SW Camera and Accessories	298	1	298
ACR Emergency Beacon	322	1	322
Solara Tracking Device	650	1	650
Subtotal (kilograms)			**10.5**
Total weight (kilograms)			**287.4**
Total weight per person (kilograms)			**143.7**
Total weight per person (pounds)			**316.1**

	calories/ 100 grams	Days 1-15 grams/ person/ day	Days 1-15 calories/ person/ day	Days 1-15 total grams for team, Days 1-15	Days 16-35 grams/ person/ day	Days 16-35 calories/ person/ day	Days 16-35 total grams for team, Days 16-35	Days 36-55 grams/ person/ day	Days 36-55 calories/ person/ day	Days 36-55 total grams for team, Days 36-55
BREAKFAST										
Pemmican	644	80	515	2,400	80	515	3,200	80	515	3,200
Rice, Instant	363	50	182	1,500	50	182	2,000	50	182	2,000
Whole Milk, Dry	600	20	120	600	40	240	1,600	40	240	1,600
Freeze-dried Cheddar Cheese	614	15	92	450	50	307	2,000	50	307	2,000
Butter	716	0	0	0	30	215	1,200	30	215	1,200
Fiber	400	12	48	360	12	48	480	12	48	480
Maple Sugar	385	10	39	300	10	39	400	10	39	400
Subtotal		**187**	**995**	**5,610**	**272**	**1,545**	**10,880**	**272**	**1,545**	**10,880**
LUNCH										
Butter	716	63	451	1,890	63	451	2,520	63	451	2,520
Bacon, double smoked	650	95	618	2,850	95	618	3,800	95	618	3,800
Macadamias, Brazil Nuts, Pecans	661	130	859	3,900	130	859	5,200	130	859	5,200
Chocolate Truffles	650	200	1,300	6,000	200	1,300	8,000	300	1950	12,000
Subtotal		**488**	**3,228**	**14,640**	**488**	**3,228**	**19,520**	**588**	**3,878**	**23,520**
DINNER										
Pemmican	644	120	773	3,600	120	773	4,800	120	773	4,800
Pasta, Ramen	383	80	306	2,400	80	306	3,200	80	306	3,200
Whole Milk, Dry	600	20	120	600	60	360	2,400	60	360	2,400
Freeze-dried Cheddar Cheese	614	30	184	900	60	368	2,400	80	491	3200
Scotch	231	5.5	13	165	6	13	220	5.5	13	220
Eniva Powder Drink Powder	320	25	80	750	25	80	1,000	12.5	40	500
Muscle Milk Drink Powder	428	0	0	0	0	0	0	35	150	1400
Subtotal		**281**	**1476**	**8,415**	**351**	**1,900**	**10,515**	**393**	**2,133**	**11,790**
Totals		**956**	**5,699**	**28,665**	**1,111**	**6,673**	**40,915**	**1,253**	**7,556**	**46,190**

Total weight of food (kilograms)   **116**
Total weight of food (pounds)   **255**

Sea Ice: Dynamics and Changes, pages 68–69

Cavalieri, D. J., Parkinson, C. L., and Vinnikov, K. Y. 2003. 30-year satellite record reveals contrasting Arctic and Antarctic decadal sea ice variability. Geophysical Research Letters, 30 (18), doi: 10.1029/2003GL018031.

Clark, D. L. 1982. The Arctic Ocean and Post-Jurassic Paleoclimatology. Climate in Earth History: Studies in Geophysics. Washington, D.C.: The National Academies Press. pp. 133.

Fetterer F., Knowles K., Meier W., and Savoie M. 2002, updated 2009. Sea Ice Index. Boulder, Colo.: National Snow and Ice Data Center. Digital media.

Maykut, G. 1986. The surface heat and mass balance. In Untersteiner N (Ed.) The geophysics of sea ice. New York: Plenium.

Mulvaney, K. 2001. At the ends of the earth: a history of the polar regions. Washington, D.C.: Island Press.

Rothrock, D. A., Yu Y., and Maykut, G.A. 1999. Thinning of the Arctic sea-ice cover. Geophysical Research Letters, 26(23): 3469-3472.

Serreze, M. and Barry, R. 2005. Atmosphere-ice-ocean interactions. In the Arctic Climate Systems. Cambridge, U.K.: Cambridge University Press.

Worsley, T. R. and Herman, Y. 1980. Episodic Ice-Free Arctic Ocean in Pliocene and Pleistocene Time: Calcareous Nannofossil Evidence. Science 210: 323–325. doi: 10.1126/science.210.4467.323.

"Optimists write badly." —Paul Valéry

This book turned out to be another expedition for us, an eighteen-month voyage that required much of the same patience, discipline, and teamwork that took us to the North Pole. On that "unsupported" journey, we had a wide network of supporters that included our families, expedition staff, coworkers, and sponsors. Although it was just the two of us on the ice, it's been the people we've met and worked with along the way that have made the experience especially rewarding. This book project was no different.

Randal Hendee, John's high school creative writing teacher, now retired, patiently edited all versions of the book. His love for the intricacies of composition propelled our work from a rough assemblage of recollections to finished form. His appreciation for the humor inherent in the English language kept the editing process light and enjoyable.

Magda Romanska, of Emerson College and Harvard University, and William Huston provided invaluable insight into the pace, clarity, and depth of the plotline. Advance readers Eileen Huston, Jim Bodony, and Lynne Huston all contributed most welcome feedback.

Chris Niskanen, former outdoors editor for the *St. Paul Pioneer Press*, gave us the initial framework by crafting the book's outline along with the first draft of chapter one. Chris also wrote the material for the inside front flap.

Minnesota is a crazy place. John, Tyler, and T.C., the Twins mascot, on May 12, 2009. John and Tyler have just thrown out the first pitches. (Tyler threw a high changeup, John a fastball in the dirt.)

Courtesy Minnesota Twins

Diana Boger designed the book and the dustjacket. Her eye for the visual aspects of storytelling is noticeable on every page.

Professor Gloria Leon and Dr. Helen Findlay were generous enough to contribute sidebars written from an academic point of view.

David Owen did the finicky image editing required for photographs awash with the elusive hues of the Arctic Ocean.

We would like to thank Lee Klancher of Octane Press for his professional perspective and for putting our story out into the world; Johnna Hyde for her gracious advice on book publishing; and our proofreaders, Charles Everitt and Zac Thompson.

Thanks also go to Jack Klobucar for continuing to advocate for our ideas and projects, Douglas Cowie for his advice, Rune Gjeldnes for his inspiration and support, and Robert B. Huston for the friendliest office on Western Avenue.

We'd like to extend our deepest gratitude to our expedition sponsors: Victorinox Swiss Army, Bergans of Norway, and DeLorme. To our expedition charity partner, CaringBridge.org, thank you for believing in our project and its mission. We believe in yours.

We'd like to thank our parents and families for giving us the confidence, care, and love that have enabled us to follow our dreams, on and off the ice.

And finally, Tyler would like to thank Sarah and Ethan for putting up with him whenever he had to "work on the book," and John would like to thank Jennifer for understanding what it takes to ski to the North Pole and produce a book about it.